"Liberating Iraq' tells the story of the many Iraqis who truly did `dance in the streets` at the fall of Saddam's repressive regime and of the Americans, nearly a half million of whom helped liberate and rebuild Iraq. But it also underscores a difficult current reality, namely, the plight of the Assyrian Christians who still struggle and suffer in today's Iraq. The world must turn its eyes to and raise its voice for the protection and sustainment of this the oldest continuing Christian community in the world!"

Stuart Bowen
Special Inspector General for Iraq Reconstruction

"Amir George is an American with American sensibilities. But his grandparents were Iraqis, and he retained contact with an extended family in Iraq. And he was a Christian aid worker who spent much of the years 2003-2009 on the ground in Iraq. This afforded him a unique vantage from which to view the American war and occupation through both American eyes and Iraqi eyes. No other account of the war and its aftermath offers similar insights. In addition, Amir George brings us more vividly than anyone else the story of the Assyrian Christian community whose decimation is arguably the greatest tragedy of the Iraq war and a terrible omen for the future of the Middle East."

Joshua Muravchik
Fellow, the Johns Hopkins University School of Advanced International Studies

AMIR GEORGE

LIBERATING
IRAQ

THE UNTOLD STORY OF THE
ASSYRIAN CHRISTIANS

With a foreword by
Lieutenant General Jay Garner,
U.S. Army Retired

13-digit ISBN 978-1-939521-00-2
10-digit ISBN 1-9395210-0-9

Dedicated to the "Angels" –
The brave men and women who liberated and rebuilt Iraq

*"Assyrian Christians, the indigenous people of Iraq, the inheritors
of the ancient Mesopotamian civilization and the world's earliest
converts to Christianity are at risk of being completely eradicated
from their homeland."*

- Paul Isaac, *New York Times*

A MIR GEORGE HAS written a scholarly, poignant and personal journey of his time with the Assyrian Christians
during the build-up to the Iraqi war, the nine-year conflict,
and the U.S. withdrawal. He exposes the all-but-invisible plight
of these Christians in the country they began. In capturing this
story, Mr. George weaves three distinct but interwoven themes:

First, *Liberating Iraq* tells the evolution of Amir George's conversion from a pacifist supporter of the campaign and a belief
that Americans were always too eager to go to war and too impatient to talk. However, beginning with day one of his six-year
involvement with Iraq, he, along with many Iraqis, began to fall
in love with "the angels," his term for the U.S. military. In fact,
the book is dedicated to "The Angels," the brave men and women
who liberated and rebuilt Iraq.

Second, and this is part of the story that I experienced firsthand, *Liberating Iraq* discusses the Assyrian Christians as the

indigenous people of Iraq and their need for a homeland, something which I fully support and have from the very beginning as a way to bring stability not only to Iraq but to the whole region.

Third, the book points out that America's failure to complete the tasks in Iraq has empowered Islamic forces and deprived those that supported the U.S., thus leaving them with no choice except to accommodate their enemies. Also, Mr. George predicts that failure to succeed in Iraq sends a clear message to the remainder of the world that those who choose to believe and support us will end up alone with no one to support them.

Finally, I am doing all I can to help get a copy of *Liberating Iraq* to the American families of those who gave their lives in the Iraq War to say "thank you" to them and the nearly 500,000 who served. It is long overdue.

"We know the Americans. They are impatient. They will be with us for a few years, but then they will leave and we will be worse off than before."

-Yonaddam Kanna
Lieutenant General Jay Garner, U.S. Army Retired

THIS **IS MY** first-hand narrative as an Assyrian who spent much of the first six years of the Iraq war in Iraq observing the situation of ordinary Iraqis, especially of the Assyrian Christian minority, and of my encounters with senior and junior officials among the Americans and others assigned to Iraq as well as Iraqi officials.

My story is unique in several ways. First, I am an Assyrian born to parents who first came to Japan in 1951, following a call by General Douglas McArthur to help rebuild immediate post-war Japan, just like what was happening beginning in 2003 in Iraq. The parallels that I saw between what was happening in Iraq and some of my earliest memories and stories from my parents about post-war Japan is what prompted me to write this book. Though I went to college in the United States, I spent my earliest formative years in Japan and am bilingual in English and Japanese. Second, I first entered Iraq before the US and coalition forces invaded the country in 2003 and my views when I first arrived were those of an anti-American, Japanese-educated pacifist. Third, my complacently rigid pacifism was profoundly shaken by what I learned from my Assyrian family and the average Iraqis of just how evil the Saddam Hussein regime had been. My own relatives described brutal treatment by Saddam's thugs, and years spent in Saddam's prisons. Finally, I learned from my Assyrian relatives that they were longing for the Americans to attack.

My philosophical about-face became, thanks to the intervention of conservative American journalist Arnaud de Borchgrave, something of a short-term media event. One of my articles written within days of the beginning of the liberation of Iraq was for several weeks on the website of the White House. This book tells my journey from pacifist to supporter of the campaign to liberate Iraq, as well as the back story of my earlier, strange encounters as a Japan-raised youth with America.

During the months and years I spent in Iraq during the war, I along with many Iraqis were repeatedly frustrated by what we saw as the UN and other officialdom's refusal to pay attention to Iraq's most important and threatened community, the ten percent of the population who were Assyrian Christians. We were offended by what we considered the eagerness on the part of some American officials to cozy up to Iraq's zealous Islamist community. Iraqis were upset by the constant reporting of bad news in the media while none of the good news, including the dramatic changes taking place in the country, ever seemed to get reported. We all watched as the nation was being transformed from an oppressive police state to a place where, for the first time in their memory, the Iraqi people were free. There seemed to be a deliberate refusal by much of the media in the country to report accurately what was happening on the ground in Iraq; that is, the transformation for the good of Iraqi society by the American presence and that of almost 50 other coalition members was palpable.

At the same time, I along with Iraqis in general, the "silent" majority," greatly cheered and were charmed by the ordinary Americans we came across in Iraq who were dedicated to doing whatever they could to contribute to a new, healthy Iraq. I was repeatedly stunned by what only can be described as the "foolishness of goodness" – the often heroic civic efforts on behalf of ordinary Iraqis by US military personnel of no special professional or educational attainment.

Much of my account is impressionistic, but where I describe public events in Iraq well covered by several other journalists' accounts, there is significant confirmation of my story. I conclude *Liberating Iraq* with a ringing reaffirmation of America's mission in the world, to spread simple decency at the grass-roots, and to construct the social basis of a functioning democracy.

In light of the so called "Arab Spring," which people in the Middle East refer to as the "Islamist Winter," the enterprise in Iraq takes on even greater significance. First, it was a direct result of the liberation of Iraq that Muammar Gaddafi decided to dismantle his weapons of mass destruction. Secondly, much of the impetus for the Arab Spring came initially from a concern that the success in Iraq in bringing freedom would spread to other parts of the Arab world, putting a damper on the Islamist designs for the area. But the failure to complete the task in Iraq and pull out far too early emboldened the Islamist forces throughout the area while also causing the "good guys" that no longer was America there to support them and that the only way forward was to make accommodations with their enemies. What America did in Iraq was right, it was honorable, and can still be salvaged if America once again lets the region and the world know that she stands behind and supports freedom and democracy and the rule of law. The often quoted ambivalence towards America comes from a completely different source. The Iraqis like all of us fell in love with America, but became frustrated when the discussions went something like, "You don't want to become like us!" to which the Americans would say, "No, we do want to become like you." Probably the best way to describe it would be the feeling towards the person that you fell in love with who ended the relationship on the basis that he or she wasn't good enough for you. It left the Iraqis and much of the region with the frustration of having seen and experienced the dream, and then seeing it cut short and having to face the stark reality of life in a troubled region. What happened in the Arab Spring was precisely what happened in Iran previously, where the "bad guys" used the "good guys" to start the revolution and then ended up taking it over and making the situation worse. A failure to succeed in Iraq is not just limited to Iraq. It sends a clear message to the rest of the world that they are on their own, with nobody to help them or support them.

Finally, as has happened so many times throughout the world in places like Korea, Japan, Europe, even though the political strategy does not always get it right, it is the young men and women of America who are so often referred to as "angels" in the form of military, peace corps, and faith based endeavors that have and continue to give hope to the world. Just like Alexis de Tocqueville said in the book *Democracy in America* in 1835,

"America is great because she is good. And if America ever ceases to be good, she will cease to be great." Whereas mistakes might have been made in the technical policy areas, over half a million of America's best and brightest loved a country that will never be the same.

I WAS WRONG

OW DO YOU admit you were wrong? What do you do when you realize those you were defending in fact did not want your defense and wanted something completely different from you and from the world? This is my story. It will probably upset everybody—those with whom I have fought for peace all my life and those for whom the decision for war comes a bit too fast. I am an Assyrian. I was born and raised in Japan where I am the second generation after my parents came to Japan in answer to General Douglas Macarthur's call for 10,000 young people to help rebuild Japan following the war. Due to my personal convictions I have always been against war for any and all reasons. It was precisely this moral conviction that led me to do all I could to stop the current war in Iraq. From participating in demonstrations against the war in Japan to strongly opposing it on my radio program, on television, in print—all in Japanese, I did my best to stand against what I thought to be an unjust war against an innocent people—in fact my people. As an Assyrian I was told the story of our people from a young age. How my grandparents had escaped the great Assyrian Genocide in 1917 settling finally in Chicago.

Currently there are approximately six million Assyrians—approximately 2.5 million in Iraq and the rest scattered in the Assyrian Diaspora across the world. Without a country or rights even in our native land, it has been the prayer of generations that the Assyrian Nation will one day be restored and the people of the once great Assyrian Empire will once again be home. It was with that feeling, together with supplies for our church and family that I went to Iraq to do all I could to help make a difference. The feeling as I crossed the border was exhilarating—home at last, I thought, as I would for the first time visit the land of my forefathers. The kindness of the border guards when they learned I was Assyrian, the taxi, the people on the street—it was like being back home after a long absence. Now I finally knew myself! The laid back, relaxed atmosphere, the kindness of strangers, the food, the smells, the language all seemed to trigger a long lost memory somewhere in my deepest DNA. The first order of business was to attend church. It was here where my morals were raked over the coals and I was first forced to examine them in the harsh light of reality.

Following a beautiful "Peace" to welcome the Peace Activists in which even the children participated, we moved to the next room to have a simple meal and conversation. Sitting next to me was an older man who carefully began to sound me out. Apparently feeling the freedom to talk in the midst of the mingling crowd he suddenly said, "There is something you should know. We didn't want to be here tonight," he said. "When the Priest asked us to gather for a Peace Service, we said we didn't want to come." I didn't understand and told him so.

"We didn't want to come because we don't want peace," he replied.

"What in the world do you mean?" I asked. "How could you not want peace?"

"We don't want peace. We want the war to come," he continued.

"What in the world are you talking about?" I blurted back. That was the beginning of a strange odyssey that deeply shattered my convictions and moral base, but at the same time gave me hope for my people and, in fact, hope for the world. Beginning that night and continuing on in the private homes of relatives with whom I stayed, little by little the scales began to come off my eyes.

I had not realized but soon learned that all foreigners in Iraq are subject to 24-hour surveillance by government "minders" who arrange all interviews, visits and contact with ordinary Iraqis. Through some fluke, probably my family connection, I was not subject to any government minders at any time throughout my stay in Iraq. As far as I know, I was the only person including the media, human shields, and others in Iraq without a government minder.

What emerged was something so awful that it is difficult even now to write about. Discussing with the head of our tribe what I should do, as I wanted to stay in Baghdad with our people during their time of trial, I was told that I could most help the Assyrian cause by going out and telling the story to the outside world. Simply put, those living in Iraq—the common, regular people—are in a living nightmare. I saw firsthand the look of terror on the faces of my family whenever there was an unknown visitor, telephone call, or knock at the door. I began to realize the horror they lived with every day.

Over and over I questioned them. "Why would you want war?

Why would any human being desire war?"

Their answer was quiet and measured. "Look at our lives! We are living like animals. No food, no car, no telephone, no job and, most of all, no hope."

I would marvel as my family went around their daily routine as normal as could be. Baghdad was completely serene without even a hint of war. Father would get up, have his breakfast and go off to work. The children would go to school; the old people— ten in the household—would do their daily chores.

"You cannot imagine what it is to live with war for twenty, thirty years. We have to keep up our routine or we will lose our minds," they told me. Then I began to see around me those who had lost their minds. It seemed every household had someone in a mental hospital or a family member killed in one of the many wars. Having been born and raised in Japan where in spite of sixty years of democracy it still retains vestiges of the four-hundred-year-old police state, I quickly began to catch the subtle nuances of a full blown, modern police state. I wept with family members as I shared their pain, and with great difficulty and deep soul searching began little by little to understand their desire for a war that would finally rid them of their nightmare. The terrible price paid in simple, down-to-earth ways—the family member with a son who just screams all the time, the family member who lost his wife and is unable to cope anymore, the family member going to a daily job with nothing to do, the family member with a son lost to the war, a husband lost to alcoholism. All of these people were facing a slow death; all hope was lost. The pictures of Sadaam Hussein whom people hailed in the beginning with great hope were everywhere. Sadaam Hussein with his hand outstretched. Sadaam Hussein firing his rifle. Sadaam Hussein in his Arab headdress. Sadaam Hussein in his classic

30-year-old picture—one or more of these four pictures were displayed on walls, in the middle of the road, in homes, as statues—he was everywhere! All seeing, all knowing, all encompassing. "Life is hell. We have no hope. But everything will be ok once the war is over," they told me. The bizarre desire for a war that would rid them of the hopelessness was at best hard to understand. "Look at it this way. No matter how bad it is we will not all die. We have hoped for some other way but nothing has worked. Twelve years ago it went almost all the way but failed. We cannot wait anymore. We want the war and we want it now."

When I explained to family members of the progress in the talks at the United Nations on working some sort of compromise with Iraq, I was welcomed not with joy but anger.

"No, there is no other way! We want the war! It is the only way he will get out of our lives."

Once again going back to my Japanese roots I began to understand. The stories I had heard from older Japanese of how in a strange way they had welcomed the sight of the bombers in the skies over Japan. At the time, I had been demonstrating against the war, thinking I was doing it for the very people I was living with; and yet I had not ever bothered to ask them what they wanted. Of course nobody wanted to be bombed, but the first sight of the American B29 bombers signaled to them that the war would soon be over. An end was in sight. There would be terrible destruction. They might very well die; but finally in a tragic way there was finally hope.

It was clear now what I should do. I began to talk to the so-called human shields. "Have you asked the people here what they want? Have you talked to regular people, away from your minder and asked them what they want?" I asked. I was shocked at the response.

"We don't need to do that. We know what they want," was the usual reply before a minder stepped up to check who I was. With tears streaming down my face as I lay in bed in a tiny house in Baghdad, crowded in with ten others of my own flesh and blood, all exhausted after another day of not living but existing without hope, exhausted in the daily struggle simply to not die, I had to say to myself, "I was wrong." How dare I claim to speak for those whom I had never even asked what they wanted!

Then I began a strange journey to do all I could as asked by my tribe and let the world know of the true situation in Iraq. Carefully and with great risk, not just for me but for all of those who told their story and opened up their homes for the camera. In every case, I did my best to tape their plight as honestly and simply as I could. Whether I could get that precious tape out of the country was a different story.

What I was not prepared for was the sheer terror they felt at speaking out. Wanting to make sure I was not simply getting the feelings of a long oppressed minority—the Assyrians—I spoke to dozens of people. Over and over again I was told, "We could be killed for speaking like this," and finding out that they would only speak in a private home or where they were absolutely sure through the introduction of another Iraqi that I was not being attended by a minder. From a former member of the Army, to a person working with the police, to taxi drivers, to store owners, to mothers, to government officials, without exception when allowed to speak freely the message was the same: "Please bring on the war. We are ready. We have suffered long enough. We may lose our lives but some of us will survive and for our children's sake please, please end our misery."

On the final day I was there, I saw the signs of war. For the first time sandbags began appearing at various government buildings;

but the solders putting them in place gave a clear message they dare not speak. They hated it. They despised it. It was their job, but they made it clear in the way they worked that they were on the side of the common people and they would not fight. As the end of my time in Iraq neared, a family member brought word that guns had just been provided to the members of the Baath Party. Another sign of war.

"But what of your feelings towards the United States and Britain?" I asked my family. Those feelings were clearly mixed. They had no love for the British or the Americans; yet, they trusted them.

"We are not afraid of the American bombing. They will bomb carefully and not purposely target the people. What we are afraid of is Saddam Hussein and what he and the Baath Party will do when the war begins. But even then, we want the war. It is the only way to escape our hell. Please tell them to hurry. We have been through war so many times, but this time it will give us hope."

The final call for help came at the most unexpected place—the border. Sent off by the crying members of my family I sadly left. Things were changing by the hour—the normally $100 ride from Baghdad to Amman was first $300 then $500 and by nightfall $1,000. Waiting to find a car to leave the country, I happened to bump into a friend from Japan's Kyodo News Agency who had room in his GMC. This was the same friend who had saved me earlier from a gang of terrorists as I waited outside the Green Zone for my ride. Then, like now, he was taking me to safety.

As we came to the border we began the routine paperwork and then prepared for the search of our vehicle. Everything was going well until suddenly the border guard asked if I had any money. We had been carefully instructed to make sure we only carried

$300 when we crossed the border, so I opened up the pouch that carried my passport and money stuffed in my shorts. Suddenly the guard began to pat me down. "Oh, no!" I thought. "It's all over." We had been told of what happened if you got caught with videotape, a cellular telephone, or any kind of electronic equipment that had not been declared. A trip back to Baghdad, a likely appearance before a judge, in some cases a 24-48-hour holding and more. He immediately found the first videotape stuffed in my pocket and took it out. I could see the expression of terror on the driver's face as he stifled a scream. The guard shook his head as he reached into my pocket and took out another tape, and then from pocket after pocket he found more tapes, a cellular telephone, a computer camera—all the forbidden things. As we stood there in sheer terror, for a brief moment I experienced what my precious family members as well as what every Iraqi had felt not for a moment but day and night, 24 hours a day, 365 days a year. That terrible feeling that your life is not yours; that your fate rests in someone else's hands to be determined by the whim of the moment. As the guard slowly laid out the precious video tape on the desk we all knew we would be taken back to Baghdad and to the beginning of a nightmare. Suddenly he laid the last videotape down and looked up. His face is frozen in my memory but it was to me the look of sadness, anger and then a final look of quiet satisfaction as he clinically shook his head and without a word returned all the precious videotape—the cry of those without a voice—to me. He didn't have to say anything. I had learned the language of the imprisoned Iraqis. Forbidden to speak by sheer terror they used the one language they had left—human kindness. As he slowly returned each tape to me, he said in his own way what my uncle had said, what the taxi driver had said, what the broken old man had said, what the man in the restaurant had said, what the Army man had said, what the man working for the police had said, what the old woman had said, what the young girl had said—he said it for them in the one last message as I crossed the border from tyranny to freedom: *Please take these tapes and show them to the world. Please help us . . . and please hurry!*

This was March 17, 2003, just three days before the American-led assault on Iraq that liberated the country from the evil regime of Saddam Hussein. I had arrived in Iraq in the last ten days of January on a family visa in place of my father. Dad was an Assyrian Christian who had been a missionary in Japan since 1951 but had visited Iraq many times in the previous decade or more to give encouragement to his Assyrian relatives. He was unwell before this scheduled trip, so he asked me to stand in for him.

I was eager to do so, and just as eager to do everything I could to stop the war that was clearly imminent. I had been born and raised in Japan, a country in which pacifism is almost a national religion. In fact, to be born and raised in Japan is to be a born and raised a pacifist. Bilingual in both English and Japanese, I'd participated in numerous demonstrations in Tokyo against war in general. I'd grown up in a country where, as a small child, some of my earliest memories were of Japanese soldiers returning home without an arm or leg during World War II. Many sat playing accordions in front of train stations begging for help. Passersby would stop and give a few coins as they felt sorry for these young men who had been abused by the tiny military clique that had destroyed their nation.

It is hard for outsiders today to understand, given Japan's prosperous, gleaming cities and reputation for innovation and modernity, but Japan was totally and completely destroyed by war. The cabal of militarists who had come to dominate Japanese politics in the 1920's and 1930's had turned a peaceful and gentle nation into a monster that ravaged Asia. The war started by Japan in Asia in the 1930's and then launched against the United States in 1941 brought a two-fold destruction to Japan. More than two million Japanese soldiers were estimated to have lost their lives in the actual fighting across Asia.

The atomic bomb detonations seared the soul of the country and turned it resolutely pacifist. But in addition, the Japanese people who had been so cruelly exploited by their military rulers turned on the military as an institution with great fury. Article Nine of the Japanese constitution of 1947 expressly forbids Japan from using military force as an instrument of national policy. Indeed, in a speech introducing the new constitution, General Douglas MacArthur, who presided over the post-war occupation of Japan, made this declaration. "I am a military man," he said. "I have dedicated my life to the military. I am overjoyed at this new Japanese constitution. It is my dream and hope that this constitution will serve as a model for the world, and that nations throughout the world will adopt it. It is my hope and prayer that as a result, war will cease and men like me – dedicated – will disappear."

This was the spirit of the generation in which I was raised. I hated even the sight of a military uniform. I felt I should be against war for any and all reasons. I felt that the clear message of the Bible was, "Thou shalt not kill." Along with the majority of all Japanese, I believed that the Americans were always too eager to go to war and too impatient to talk. I reconciled my beliefs about the wickedness of war with denominations like the Mennonites that have historically opposed warfare, even in self-defense.

My commitment was to what I called "Preventive Diplomacy"

and I wrote of it in nearly all of my books and spoke about it in hundreds of speeches throughout the country. I expressed the view that Japan was a beacon of peace, committed to diplomacy instead of war. One of my dear friends for over 20 years has been the Mayor of Hiroshima, and is a strong proponent of the view that peace must be preserved at all costs.

Before setting off for Iraq, I'd taken part in demonstrations against US war plans in the center of Tokyo. I'd written forcefully against the war in opinion columns for Japanese-language newspapers. I'd also been outspoken in arguing against the forthcoming war on Japanese TV talk shows. I thought any war by the US against Iraq would be an unjust war against an innocent people. In fact, I thought any war would be a war also against my own people, the Assyrians.

I'd been told as a boy about the Great Assyrian Genocide of 1915-1917 from which my grandparents had barely escaped before settling in Chicago. There are believed to be about six million Assyrians in the world today, but only some 2.5 million of them live in Iraq, though about half of the Assyrians outside the country have fled there since the war began in 2003. The remainder are scattered throughout a widely dispersed global diaspora. It's been the prayer of millions of Assyrians that the Assyrian nation will one day be restored and that the descendants of those who built the great Assyrian Empire will one day return home. Now, it seemed, the Americans were going to crush all those dreams in their assault upon Iraq.

I had been harboring these thoughts when I flew into Amman, Jordan the third week of January 2003 and secured a vehicle to transport humanitarian supplies and some boxes of medicines that an official at the Iraqi embassy in Tokyo had requested I bring in. The long drive across the desert of eastern Jordan had been bumpy and wearying and I was nervous about the reception I would get at the Iraqi border as an American. I made the trip along with members of a Japanese humanitarian aid team, the Japan Emergency Team, an organization that I had founded a few years before.

Though I thought that most Iraqis would welcome my anti-war credentials, I was frankly concerned about how they would view foreigners arriving in the country. But I needn't have worried about how I would be received. The kindness of ordinary, low-level Iraqi officials at the border-crossing was overwhelming, especially when they learned that I was Assyrian. Entering Baghdad for the first time, however, I was shocked at the extensive security. We passed through seven checkpoints just to get into the city. In spite of the imminent threat of war, there was no tension at all in Baghdad itself.

The first night I stayed in the home of the family of the official at the Iraqi embassy in Tokyo who had asked me to bring in boxes of medicines for him. The next day, I located at the UN headquarters in Baghdad thanks to one of my former students from a course I had taught in Japan. He proved extremely helpful because he made it possible for me to visit the UN offices, use the Internet, and begin the search for my relatives, the ones my father had met on previous visits to Iraq. At the UN I serendipitously met an Assyrian Iraqi who actually knew my family and arranged for me to meet them. The relatives included an uncle, George, who, with his wife, had three grown children who had their own children. The house he lived in was in the Al Mansour district of Baghdad. It was a modest, two-story house with bedrooms on the main and first floors. Uncle George was over 60 years old, of medium height, and rather paunchy, as many Middle Eastern men of a certain age can be. For years he had worked at the Iraqi

Oil Company, but was now retired. His daughter Mary, in her thirties, a quiet and shy woman who seemed to carry about with her burdensome memories, had previously worked for the Iraqi Foreign Ministry as a diplomat. What had happened to her was one of a series of hammer-like facts that, soon after my arrival in Iraq, assaulted my naïve preconceptions of life in Iraq and forced me to change my mind completely about the war.

I certainly wasn't the only foreigner in Iraq that February who was dead set against the war. Saddam Hussein, in a desperate effort to stave off the coming cataclysm, had invited in several idealistic Westerners as human shields. These men and women, often in their sixties and seventies who were members of liberal-inclined church groups such as the Methodists and the Mennonites—who have traditionally been against war—volunteered to place themselves around strategic military and civilian targets in Baghdad. Their naïve hope was that the presence of helpless foreign civilians in the middle of a war zone might deter American war planners from targeting the locations. The human shields were mainly British and American, and they were quick to let you know how much they detested the governments of their own countries. For all of them, war was the worst possible eventuality for Iraq. But, as I was to quickly discover, this wasn't at all the view of many of the Iraqis I had an opportunity to talk with. More years of living under Saddam Hussein was what they feared more than anything.

The Iraqi government wasted no time in organizing a church event to accommodate the idealism of the human shields and to present a propaganda picture of overwhelming Iraqi and international solidarity against the impending American attack. It took place eight days after I arrived in Baghdad, and it was a government-organized anti-war rally of the human shields and selected

Iraqi citizens that was to be held in a large church in Baghdad. I decided to go, for I had met several Assyrian Christians since arriving in the country, and some of them were going to be there.

Shortly before 7 o'clock in the evening, I arrived at a large church in the Dora district of Baghdad. The church was the seat of the Metropolitan of Baghdad, Mar Gewargis ("Mar" is often used by senior Church of the East clerics to indicate respect for their piety), and he had been asked by the Iraqi government to address the foreign arrivals and greet them in the name of the government of Iraq. After milling around for a while, we all trooped into the church for the service and the talk by an Assyrian church official.

The church was filled with human shield idealists as well as a sprinkling of Iraqis whose faces didn't express the open friendliness of the foreigners. These were the Iraqi minders, government stooges who were routinely assigned to almost every foreign delegation visiting Iraq to ensure that only certain places were visited, only certain people spoken to, and that nothing even remotely critical of Saddam Hussein or his regime was uttered by anyone, even a foreigner. As far as I knew, I might have been the only foreigner in Baghdad at the time without a minder. This was because I had been given a family visa for a family visit by the Iraqi embassy in Tokyo.

There were also present, however, many Assyrian church members, members of Baghdad's Christian community who might normally be in such a church on any given Sunday for a church service. Sitting next to me in the church was an older man, judging by his features an Assyrian rather than an Iraqi Arab, who began to sound me out quietly during the service about my views. Nothing about his manner or the clothes he was wearing marked him to be other than an ordinary Assyrian member of the church. But the words he whispered to me, staring straight ahead all the while as he spoke, shocked me.

"There is something you need to know," he said, half turning to be sure that I was listening. "None of us wanted to be here. When the priest asked us to attend a peace service, we said that we didn't want to come."

"What in the world do you mean?" I hissed back under my breath. "How could you not want peace?"

"We don't want peace," he said, looking straight ahead, desperately fearful that he might be noticed speaking to me by one of the government minders who were prominent throughout the church congregation. "We want the war to come."

I was dumbfounded. Here I was, proud of the fact that I had bravely come to Baghdad to try to forestall an American attack, and I was being told by the very people I thought I was protecting that they wanted the war to happen.

After the church service concluded we all made our way into a church hall on the other side of an open space that adjoined the church. White tablecloths covered the tables which were laden with delicious Iraqi dishes: chicken, lamb, eggplant, potatoes, spring onions, fish and copious helpings of rice. Although it wasn't an elaborate meal, it was ample, and for those of us who hadn't eaten much in several days, it was a feast. While we stood in line to serve ourselves buffet-style, I struggled to make sense of what I had just been told. I needed to talk to some of the human shields.

"Have you talked to ordinary people here?" I asked. "Have you been able to ask them what they want to see happen, without a minder present?"

"We don't need to ask them what they want," was the haughty answer of one graying American who had volunteered. I could imagine him just a few years earlier daubed in peace symbols and splashing around in the mud of Woodstock. "We know what they want."

Right.

It was just the beginning of a shocking revelation that flooded in on my naïve mind in the next few days and weeks. These well-intentioned, but shockingly naïve idealists thought they were making a contribution to Iraq by being physically present to inhibit the war from starting. In fact, however, the ordinary Iraqis I had met overwhelmingly wanted the war to begin. By some fluke, possibly because my father had been to Iraq before and I wasn't considered dangerous by the regime, I hadn't been assigned a minder. I was thus able to talk uninhibitedly with not only Uncle George and his family, but with other Iraqi Assyrian families they introduced me to. I began to realize the sheer terror that many, perhaps most, Iraqi families lived through as they tried to cope with the totalitarian nightmare that was Saddam Hussein's Iraq. I had been completely wrong about the war and now I was forced to admit it.

It's very difficult for ordinary Americans to grasp what life is like living under a brutal, totalitarian dictatorship. We've been blessed with so much freedom for so long that it requires an imaginative leap to project ourselves into a home where all the inhabitants shake in terror when there is a knock on the door that they are not expecting. I was shocked by the look of fear that came over them if I inadvertently surprised them by bringing home someone they didn't know; or seeing everyone in the room stiffen when the phone rang.

In my uncle's family I learned first-hand about the nightmarish conditions people lived under. Uncle George's daughter, Mary, worked in a pharmacy in Baghdad. But she hadn't originally been trained as a pharmacist. She had done well enough in her studies at the University of Baghdad to be accepted into the Iraqi Foreign Service. She had been assigned in the late 1980's as a junior diplomat to Moscow where for the wrong reasons she attracted the eye of the Iraqi ambassador. He made clear his intentions very quickly, and they weren't for her to busy herself analyzing the Soviet economy. Quite simply, he wanted to sleep with her. She refused. Within a matter of days she was recalled to Baghdad and spent the next seven years in Abu Ghraib prison. Miraculously, she survived, and after Saddam's fall, she was restored to her previous rank in the Foreign Ministry as if nothing had happened. Another of my relatives, who lives in Assyria, had been a handsome young man who wanted to work for the rights of Iraq's Assyrian Christians. One night he too disappeared, and it was quickly learned that he had been spirited away into the purgatory of the Saddam-era Abu Ghraib prison. There he had received the full dosage of Saddam's tortures. When he eventually got out, the top of his forehead had a huge gash in it like Braveheart in the movie with the same name, and his body was covered with the scars inflicted by cigarette burns and other instruments of torture.

As the days went by, the scales began to fall from my eyes. I kept asking, but with diminishing conviction, "Why would you want war? Why would anyone want war?"

"Look at our lives!" they would answer. "We are living like animals. We have little food, no car, no telephone, no job, and minimal hope. You cannot imagine what it has been like to live this way for twenty or thirty years. We have been almost constantly at war with someone or other. We have to maintain a routine or we would lose our minds."

Some, indeed, had apparently lost their minds. As I visited

more and more households of my relatives and relatives' friends, I began to notice strange but disturbing sights. The walls of everyone's homes seemed to be filled with pictures of family members who had been killed in the Iran-Iraq war of 1980-1988 or the short war in the First Gulf War of 1991, or taken away, usually in the night, by Saddam's security services. Some homes seemed to have at least one family member who would have been, in many other countries, committed to a psychiatric ward. There was the pre-teenage child who for inexplicable reasons would scream at the top of his voice for hours at a time, and the adults who sat in chairs with lifeless eyes staring at the wall. I learned that some of these homes had lost family members to one or other of Saddam Hussein's murderous rampages to search for political enemies among his own population. Others had succumbed to alcoholism or to a paralyzing fear of saying or doing something that might displease Iraq's leader, Saddam Hussein, or his army of ubiquitous informants.

Since first getting his hands on the levers of political power in Iraq in 1968—for several years he shared it with Abu Bakr—Saddam had become an all-consuming figure in Iraqi life. Faded photographs of the dictator festooned the walls of government offices, and statues in different parts of Baghdad were reminders of him. There was Saddam Hussein with his hand outstretched, Lenin-style, directing the gaze of Iraqis towards the future; Saddam Hussein firing a rifle which he held pointed in the air with just one hand; Saddam Hussein's sculptured forearms holding two gigantic, concrete scimitars forming a "victory arch" in downtown Baghdad; Saddam Hussein's photograph being greeted by a clutch of excited school children. He was everywhere. His face was even on the national banknotes.

Yet he was feared and hated more than I had ever known possible. "Life here is hell," I heard over and over again. "We have no hope. Everything will be okay after the war is over. Look at it this way. We will not all die. We have always hoped something else would put an end to our nightmare, but it has not worked that way. Twelve years ago (during the Gulf War) we almost saw it come to an end, but that didn't happen. We can't wait any more. We want war and we want it now."

I feebly tried to placate my relatives with vague possibilities of peace. Hadn't they heard about the progress of compromise talks with Iraq at the UN, I asked? Instead of being met by grateful mumblings of hope, I encountered raw anger from them. "No, there is no other way than war. We want war! It is the only way we will get our lives back." At night, lying in my bed in a small Baghdad house with ten relatives, I often let my tears come. Who was I to tell these wonderful people what was best for them? What did I really know about their lives?

At the same time, I was wrestling with my Christian faith. It had been a cornerstone of my belief that peace was the ultimate good. When I was alone in my room at night, I searched the scriptures for insights. There was clearly in the scriptures a permanent tension between good and evil. Having been brought up in the peace and prosperity of Japan and—in college and afterwards—the United States, I honestly thought that while there had clearly been evil in the not too recent past, things had changed. Of course, there had been the killing fields of Cambodia, a country to which I had taken a team for humanitarian rebuilding after a natural disaster a few years earlier. But I had never experienced firsthand the stark evil that Saddam and his sons embodied. It seemed to be a different kind of evil from anything I had experienced in real life; it was a different form of evil. What I was encountering in the terrible tales of what had happened to my family members under Saddam seemed to belong in another category. I knew about the evil that comes into existence in the wake of a war. That kind of evil at least has a logic to it. What I was encountering with the Saddam regime, however, was evil for its own sake; evil that existed because it seemed to provide the perpetrators of it with pleasure.

Now I had to deal with another issue central to my entire Christian faith. How did a Christian face evil? Did he simply capitulate to it? If evil went on expressing itself, how should a Christian act? What if we fasted and prayed and yet evil still continued to exist? What then? What should a Christian do?

I was horrified as the Assyrian I called Braveheart lifted his shirt to show me the dozens of cigarette burns and cuts across his body. I was filled with an indescribable grief as I watched Mary shuffle about, her spirit broken by her years spent inside Abu Ghraib. I could hardly compose myself as family after family showed me the black and white photos of relatives murdered by Saddam. I realized, sitting all alone in my room, that my view of evil, neat and idealistic as it had been, didn't take into account the almost tangible evil that seems to hover in the air as a complacent, malignant reality of life itself.

The relentless message that I was hearing from my relatives— war is better than what we have at present—took me back to some of my earliest memories in Japan, memories of talking to older Japanese who had lived through the B-29 fire-bombing campaign of the US Army Air Corps against Tokyo and other Japanese cities. The older Japanese I had often spoken with recalled welcoming in a strange way the sight of the B-29s droning menacingly in the sky overhead. There would be great destruction and many deaths, several older Japanese had told me, but they knew that the war would eventually be over. The nightmare of the daily struggle to survive, the sickening lies of the Japanese militarist war machine, would be gone forever. There would yet be much suffering for ordinary Japanese, but the nightmare of rule by wartime leader Hideki Tojo would be over. The Americans would surely win, and then a new reality would come upon the country.

Many Japanese all but worshiped Japan's post-war American ruler, General Douglas MacArthur. Some wept openly when the constitution was announced, as well as at the height of the Korean War, President Truman fired MacArthur for insubordination and recalled him to Washington.

I was going through a real moral crisis. All of my comfortable pacifist assumptions had crashed in flames. I knew that as a simple human being and as a Christian I was called to exert all the strength I could to stop war and advance peace. I now realized that at a certain point, when evil becomes not just a byproduct of bad behavior but an entity unto itself, it needed to be confronted directly and defeated. As a Christian, I saw my mission from God as being one to fight evil. While actual force, I felt, should always be a last resort, in the end, the only way for evil to be conquered might be for it to be physically defeated. This eventuality should never deflect a person from doing everything in his means to avoid actual physical violence against evil, but sometimes it might be necessary. The challenge for every Christian is to know when the line separating reasonable discourse with outright confrontation has to be crossed.

Finally, I also realized something else. While evil certainly exists, so does good. Men and women who had stood against Saddam Hussein with tremendous love and commitment to each other and to the idea of good would surely prevail. I knew from Scripture that where there is much evil, God's grace in providing goodness is even greater. I began to see in the Bible how the battle against evil had an end game. In the end evil fails and good triumphs. This is truly the battle of the ages and without the promise which Christian believers have that in the end good triumphs over evil it would truly be a sorry world we would all have to live in.

The comfort that settled in my heart on those lonely nights in Uncle George's house in the Mansour district of Baghdad as I finally wrenched myself through these issues was very simple. It was the quiet peace of God. Deep, deep down in my heart, I knew that good would prevail for Iraq and for my dear Assyrian Christian brothers and sisters. It has been my rallying cry ever since. Shortly after getting in touch with my family, I was taken over to meet with Mar Gewargis, who was the archbishop of Iraq. Under unbelievable circumstances, he was preserving the oldest church in the world under Saddam's nightmare. While there was severe persecution of the Assyrians, they were allowed limited freedom within the church properties. It was there that I first met the Assyrian underground and someone who would later become a dear friend. Mar Gewargis was in the middle of an extremely sensitive operation of having to protect his people and church while at the same time trying to keep basic relations with the oppressive government. There in the church's parlor was a meeting of the Assyrian underground in which they were planning how they would operate. One of the critical issues was that of the Assyrian flag, a distinctive flag that included the Tigris and Euphrates rivers and was symbolic of the Assyrian nation. During Saddam's time, they were prohibited from flying the flag or even owning it. While I was there, Mar Gewargis mentioned that he had one of the flags, in his room, that he had kept safely through all the time during the persecution by Saddam.

The Assyrian underground, known as Zowaa, or The Assyrian Democratic Movement, ran a network of cells throughout the country, protecting the Assyrians and working for the day that they would ultimately be free. Many were caught and put into the much feared Abu Ghraib prison and many had been martyred. Sitting there in the church headquarters looking at Assyrians from my own tribe who were risking their lives every day brought home the seriousness of what was taking place. One of the dreams of that time was to someday see liberation where we could actually raise the Assyrian flag, and the greeting among the Assyrians was a gesture of hoisting a flag, indicating that someday, we would raise the flag. It was only a few months later that this dream came to be. I greatly respected Mar Gewargis and one of the reasons I fought so hard to stay in Iraq was because of his example. So many had left, but he had chosen always to stay with his people.

In contrast with my face-to-face encounter with the horrible reality of evil under Saddam in Baghdad, I found myself disgusted with so many of the anti-war activists I had spent time with since arriving in Iraq. First of all, there was their intellectual dishonesty. They refused to acknowledge the fact that the people whom they were ostensibly protecting from war in fact wanted the war to come. I was in a dilemma. Should I leave right then, or should I gather more evidence of the nightmare of Iraq? I needed a wise and authoritative person to give me advice, an Iraqi whom I knew I could trust.

I found him in Baghdad at the beginning of March 2003. His name was Marcus Paulus and he was the leader of the Tiari tribe to which our family had belonged. A gentle, slow-moving man of above medium height who had spent fourteen years as an Iraqi prisoner of war of the Iranians, Marcus Paulus exhibited both a quiet dignity and a moral authority. He had been a senior officer in the Iraqi air force. In Iran he had been beaten and deliberately mistreated for the sole reason that he was known to be an Assyrian Christian. Even today he walks with a cane and a limp.

The Assyrian community of Iraq usually identifies itself according to tribal loyalties. It was Uncle George who took me to meet Marcus Paulus. He had decided that Paulus, as tribal leader, should have the last word on whether I should stay in Iraq and gather more information or leave immediately. Tribes in Iraq play an important role in providing a network of support and protection for tribal members who move around the country. We sat down and Paulus told me he knew of our family, as he had met my father before. Paulus was a courtly and kindly man, but he was very direct with me. "Stay here until you learn enough to go away and explain what life is like here," he advised me. "When you leave, tell the world the truth. That is how you can best serve our tribe."

I followed his advice carefully, filling notebooks, videotapes and tape cassettes with story after story of Saddam's Iraq. I took some risks speaking to people about matters that were not supposed to get out of Iraq, but the people I met with—often quite surreptitiously—took far more risks than I did. The worst that might happen to me was that I would be questioned for a few hours and then ordered to leave the country. For my informants, however, knowledge that they had spoken about their lives to an American might generate imprisonment, torture, or much worse. Several of my informants said, "We could be killed for speaking like this."

It certainly wasn't easy getting their stories. No one was willing to speak to me except privately in his home or in a place that he considered safe. Invariably, my informants would ask me multiple questions to ensure that I was not being watched or followed by an Iraqi government minder. Despite these necessary measures of caution, I managed to speak with a broad variety of Iraqis: former soldiers of the Iraqi army, people connected loosely to the police, cab drivers, former government officials. The message was always the same. "Please bring on the war," they begged, as if I had any power at all to influence American policy. "We are ready. We have suffered long enough. We may lose our lives but some of us will survive. For our children's sake, please end our misery."

By early March, after meeting with Marcus Paulus, I had been in Iraq some six weeks. Signs had finally begun to appear around Baghdad that the regime now considered that war might be in the offing. Sandbags began to appear in the windows of government buildings. But the soldiers placing them there gave no impression of doing so with any determination to protect the city. In fact, though they were obviously too scared to explain what they were doing. They made it abundantly clear to casual passers-by that they really didn't want to be bothered with military preparations at all. They moved slowly, almost languidly, as if eager to show that they had no enthusiasm whatever for the task of defending the regime. They were going through the motions of working, almost apologetic about clogging up the sidewalk to get the job done. They seemed to want to make it clear to everyone who was watching that the only "side" they were on was that of the ordinary people of Iraq. It seemed plain to me that when the American-led invasion started, they wouldn't put up much of a fight.

At home with Uncle George, a family member reported one evening that he had heard that rifles—almost certainly AK-47 semi-automatics—had just been handed out to members of the Baath Party, the political party that ruled Iraq. As an American, I wondered what the attitudes of ordinary Iraqis were towards Americans, and indeed towards Britons, the two nationalities that would be foremost in the assault upon the Saddam Hussein regime.

Talking to the average Iraqis, all spoke about when Iraq was at its best. That was the period when the British were in Iraq. The British were on nobody's favorite-country list either. The British, after all, had been the colonial rulers of Baghdad after World War 1, and even after Iraq gained official independence in the 1930's, Britain continued to have military bases in the country. It was literally after the British left that everything went bad, and the Iraqis, even today, look back wistfully at the time when the British and the Iraqi king ruled. Nevertheless, I had the unmistakable impression that everyone wanted the Americans to begin attacking. My host George Toma expressed the sentiment most succinctly, though I also heard similar feelings expressed by Iraqi UN workers and many others. "We are not afraid of the American bombing," he said, as though a veteran eyewitness of innumerable USAir Force bombing runs. "They will bomb carefully and they will not deliberately target civilians. What we are all most scared about is Saddam and what he will do when the war begins. He may throw his chemical and biological weaponry into the struggle. Still, we want the war to come. It will be the only way we can escape this living nightmare. We have been through war plenty of times in the past. We know what it is like. Please tell them to hurry."

But who was I to tell anyone, especially the US government, to do anything? Was I supposed to have a direct line to the White House to inform President Bush not to waste another moment before starting the war? I was tempted to laugh at these suggestions, except that the earnestness of everyone who spoke in this vein was transparent. Did they really imagine that I was in a position to influence events?

I had by now been in Iraq more than six weeks. Some of the people I spoke to were increasingly desperate for the war to begin. The feeling in Baghdad was that if the Americans and British did not come, there was going to be a mass suicide. People could not stand it anymore. My Uncle George looked at me and said, "Look, we can't live like this anymore. We live like animals. My son goes every day to school and studies about Saddam. Every TV channel is Saddam. Saddam is on the money, he is on the wall. We dream about Saddam. We know that the Americans and the British are not going to purposely kill people, but it is the only way to get rid of this hell that we live in. I would gladly die if it meant that my family could finally be free."

Two days later, I realized that I must now leave Baghdad as quickly as possible. Some of the human shields had opted for discretion as the better part of valor and already had left the country, despite their proud boasts on entering the country that they were going to help prevent the war from breaking out. My own Assyrian relatives were becoming more and more worried for me, and kept urging me to make preparations for my departure.

I had originally come into Iraq by road with a small quantity of humanitarian supplies. At this stage of things, the only way to leave Iraq was by road into Jordan. My Uncle George told me he thought it was better if I left. I didn't want to because I felt that it was unfair to leave when things got tough and return when they became better. I wanted to be there during the bombing and the difficult time because only then would I have the standing to really help. My Uncle George insisted that we once again meet with Marcus Paulus, the head of our tribe. We went to his house, which was a large house in the nicest part of Baghdad. As we waited for him to come out, several bodyguards gave us strange looks. Finally he came out accompanied by two additional body-guards, and I can say it reminded me of the Japanese mafia. My uncle explained that he felt that it was starting to get very dangerous and he thought it was better that I left. Marcus asked me what I thought, and I tried to make the case that I wanted to stay. Many Iraqi people had left the country and were resented for it. I didn't want to do the same thing because I wanted to have credibility with the people I wanted to help. Then Marcus said, "Let me make my decision," and left the room for about twenty minutes. When he returned, he said to me, "I have made my decision. It is best for our tribe if you go because we need someone on the outside to explain our situation and we don't know how things are going to develop. You could help us more from outside the country. Marcus Paulus virtually ordered me out of Iraq. I reluctantly accepted his decision. I had during my several weeks in Iraq grown very close to George Toma and his extended family, and many of them were crying as I packed my things. On March 17, 2003, one of my cousins drove me to the Palestine Hotel, the last location in Baghdad where there were taxis for hire to drive out to the Iraqi-Jordanian border. Waiting around, I happened to meet a friend and his colleagues from Kyodo News. I asked if they had room for another passenger and they did, so they let me ride with them in their GMC that they had chartered to take them to Amman.

People often say that the market understands things better than anything else. As journalists, UN personnel, NGO representatives, diplomats and other foreigners still in Iraq decided that it was now time to quit the country, prices for the journey across the desert to Amman skyrocketed, first by the day, then by the hour. The normal price for the Amman ride was $100, but on the morning when I was due to leave it had risen to $300. By nightfall it had soared to $1,000. I was lucky to secure a place in a taxi with a friend from Japan's Kyodo News Agency and three of his colleagues. There were five of us passengers crammed into an aging Mercedes with as much luggage as we had dared to bring into Iraq and to take out.

Just before we set off, as we were securing our luggage in the trunk, I recognized the former AP and CNN reporter Peter Arnett. A little like a vulture circling over the location of a future battle, he had arrived in Baghdad to cover the war and to be in Baghdad when the first American bombs started falling. In February, 1991, he had crouched behind a window in the Palestine Hotel when the Americans had unleashed Desert Storm. Peter Arnett had, of course, survived. Now he had returned to his erstwhile reporting hot-spot as a reporter for Al Jazeera TV, the Qatar-based satellite TV news organization widely watched throughout the Arab world. As my Japanese colleagues and I tried to squeeze luggage into every available space in the GMC, I filled Peter in on much of the street talk I had heard from my relatives, including the fact that most Iraqis with whom I had spoken were really eager to see the approaching war get under way. He said he agreed that it was true they probably did, but his own employers of the moment—Al Jazeera—were decidedly against the war and probably wouldn't want to hear him reporting like that. He smiled as we parted and he gave me a shrug as if to say, "Well, that's my job and I chose it."

After grabbing a quick bite to eat, we settled into the car in near-silence and started the long and wearying drive to the Jordanian border at around 1.00 p.m. We made a couple of rest stops or so and bought some snacks en route, but didn't make it to the checkpoint on the Iraqi side of the border with Jordan until 9.00 p.m. We were all slightly frazzled and bone-tired from the excitement over leaving and the jarring journey on poorly-maintained roads.

Everybody in the car was nervous about the process of exiting Iraq. We had been carefully instructed by foreigners who had made this journey before not to take out of Iraq more than $300 in cash. The Iraqi border officials would, we had been told, be suspicious if we had a large amount of US dollars on us when we left the country. They might suspect us of exchanging dollars on the black market—or worse.

But in the end, the generous honesty of one Iraqi border guard ensured that we all got out safely; in my case, with an amazing story to tell.

CHAPTER TWO

MY FORMATIVE YEARS

SOME PEOPLE SAY that I am more Japanese than American. I certainly look American. I am five feet ten inches tall, have light-brown hair, and nothing else about my physical features says Japanese. But Japanese was my first language growing up, I speak Japanese bilingually, and in some ways I think like a Japanese. In fact, it was the Japanese way of thinking about war that led me to Iraq as an ardent foe of American military intervention in that country. But I am getting ahead of myself.

My father was born in Chicago, the son of a couple who had immigrated to the United States after fleeing the terrible attacks against the Assyrians of Iraq that took place in 1915. He attended high school in the suburbs of Chicago, and then went on to Bob Jones University, Moody Bible College in Chicago, and the Winona Lake School of Theology in Winona Lake, Indiana. He'd come to faith in Christ at an outdoor rally with Charles E. Fuller at Soldier Field in Chicago—a place made famous

by evangelist Billy Graham, among others, when he was working for Youth for Christ, and met Reverend Graham's precious
mother who was a counselor at the event.

What happened in his college years at Bob Jones University
in South Carolina was what changed his life forever. Barely a
month after the Japanese surrendered to US forces aboard the
battleship USS Missouri in Yokohama Bay, General Douglas
MacArthur, SACP (Supreme Allied Commander Pacific), sat
down with a group of four American clergymen. An Episcopa-
lian himself, MacArthur took seriously the task assigned to him
by President Truman as commander of the American occupation
of Japan. He was going to try to remold the entire Japanese psy-
che after its perversion by the forces of militarism during the war
years. He asked the clergy to send out a call to 10,000 American
missionaries to come over to Japan and help the nation recover.
He thought that devout American Christians could import into
Japan not only the ideas of Christianity, but instincts for democracy as well.

His appeal for 10,000 missionaries fell on fertile soil when it
was transmitted to Christian colleges and churches across the
United States. A generation of young people responded to the
challenge and flocked into postwar Japan. They started schools,
hospitals, institutions for the needy and a host of other organizations and institutions. They transformed postwar Japan.

Among them, quite independently of each other, were both
my parents. My mother, born and raised in the border area of
Montana and North Dakota, had come to faith as a child and
had gone on to attend Prairie Bible Institute in Three Hills, Al-
berta in Canada.

When I used to ask my dad what really prompted him to dig
up his roots, leave Chicago, perhaps forever, and head over to

Japan, his response was typical of that attitude of the "Greatest Generation," the generation that fought World War II heroically with an "aw shucks" view of their own heroism. It was Tom Brokaw's best-selling book, *The Greatest Generation,* that led to the widespread adoption of the phrase to apply to the young American men and women who threw themselves into the struggle against Nazi Germany and Japanese militarism with quite heroic absence of self-consciousness. "Because they needed us," was his reply. The "they" were the Japanese, defeated, humiliated, destitute, and needing some encouragement from anyone who took the trouble to offer it. "Things were terrible here," he said, thinking back to just how primitive and impoverished life was after World War II, "and they needed us." Yet my father, in offering this explanation, would invariably fail to mention how many people had been against his coming to Japan as a missionary. Americans were still bitter about the Japanese because of the war Japan had started and many thought that the last thing any American should do was to come to Japan and be a missionary.

My dad sailed from San Francisco aboard the President Wilson and arrived in Tokyo's port, Yokohama. The ship docked on May 5, 1952. Initially, my dad stayed in the Shizuoka district south of Tokyo and concentrated on learning Japanese. Not long afterwards, he scraped together some money, bought a very simple motor-home, and began crisscrossing Japan and holding evangelistic meetings with an assistant. During these trips he came to love the Japanese people, the language, and their country. One of the joys of my life is that when I speak throughout Japan almost invariably someone will come up afterwards and say, "I think your father came to our town many years ago," so I get to see where he had travelled. At the time, many Japanese had been so hurt and disillusioned by where their country's militaristic leaders had led them that they were surprisingly open to the Christian message. Gradually, however, as Japan began to grow more prosperous, the memories of their society's material and spiritual destitution in the 1940's were eclipsed by a rising tide of prosperity, national confidence, and even complacency. Today, the total number of Japanese describing themselves as Christian is, according to a Gallup poll conducted a few years ago, more than six percent. I believe that this figure testifies to the deep influence the generation of young, idealistic Americans had in transforming a country destroyed by war, much as they were to do later on in Iraq as we all watched.

My dad, on arriving in Japan as an earnest young Christian, took very seriously the advice of the Apostle Paul to try and stay away from marriage. He even started a small, informal club, composed of fellow-missionaries, called Bachelors till the Rapture, dedicated to the idea that serious young missionary men shouldn't waste time on forming families. One of his financial supporters in the missionary effort, however, thought this was a poor idea for a young missionary in an unfamiliar cultural environment. This benefactor also happened to know my mother as well. Trying to engineer a meeting between them, he insisted that my dad meet her as her ship came in at Yokahama. He must have assumed that Cupid would be present at such an encounter.

To the considerable annoyance of the supporter, my father failed to obey the request and missed my mother completely when she first arrived in Yokahama in 1954. It wasn't until months later at a missionary training center in Karuizawa, a famous resort in the hills outside Tokyo, that my parents first met. Karuizawa itself had been founded by missionaries in 1886 and for years Western missionaries had established a spiritual retreat and training center there. After sweating through a Japanese summer in the days before air-conditioning, my dad had been only too happy to take a break at a cool hill-station retreat away from his regular routine. He had been invited to speak at the retreat center. My mother, as it happened, was listening in the back of the room. When the talk was over she was introduced to him. They started courting, and within a short time both fell in love.

They had met at Karuizawa, and this is where they got married within a year of their original meeting. My mother was given away by her Aunt Alma Aarhus who was a fellow missionary on Taiwan. My parents spent their honeymoon at the resort town of Atami. It was a romantic combination, to have met and later married at Karuizawa and then to have honeymooned at Atami.

Since beginning my own professional life in Japan, I find myself once or twice a year in Atami speaking at some function or other. I always feel a special emotional tug whenever I am there. What has given me a special joy is often after a speech somewhere or other in Japan, I often meet a Japanese who first heard my dad speak at a meeting years before and, as a result of listening to what my dad had to say, had a spiritual renewal in his or her own life.

We lived very differently from the families of most of the other Western missionaries in Japan. Many Westerners, especially Americans, looked down on the Japanese. After all, we were reminded, they had started the war, they were "pagans," they probably had all sorts of dangerous infectious diseases, and they might mislead young foreigners growing up among them. Some missionary families even prohibited their own children from playing with Japanese kids. This was not at all, however, my dad's attitude. To their everlasting credit, neither my father nor my mother ever shared this attitude. First of all, unlike the apparent majority of foreigners living in Japan, my dad had taken the trouble to learn Japanese well. He spoke it fluently and he greatly admired Japanese culture. He considered Japanese people not only in general better mannered than Americans, but actually a lot smarter. It was we Americans, my dad insisted, who needed to learn from the Japanese, not the other way round.

My three brothers and I grew up completely bilingual. In fact, at home we often spoke an eclectic mixture of colloquial Japanese and colloquial English. "Go to the *Eki* (train station)," my dad or mom would say, "and get *hyaku gramu* (100 grams) of *hikiniku* (hamburger meat), and stop by the *yaoya* (vegetable store) and get a plate of *kyuri* (cucumbers). And *hayaku shiro!*" ("hurry up!") At home we would eat Japanese food with chopsticks. We children assumed that this was the way everyone ate, everywhere in the world.

It was thus a great shock when I was six years old and I visited the United States for the first time. To begin with, compared with the Japanese, everyone seemed so large. In the early years after World War II, most Japanese were of much smaller stature than most Americans. Not only were Americans huge, I thought as I watched them in restaurants, but they ate gargantuan servings of food. I was astounded by the tremendous hamburgers and large servings of fries, the gallon-sized (or so it seemed) milkshakes, the waste of so many things. My mother did her best to make apologies for us all, since our American relatives believed we youngsters were "growing up with pagans." But just being in America was a shattering experience for us. One day, we sort of spontaneously rebelled against the knives and forks and huge quantities of food served, and simply took out our chopsticks and started eating with them. At the same time, we reverted to speaking Japanese with each other.

It didn't help. In no time, we realized that people were simply laughing at us openly. Embarrassed, we gave up the chopsticks and the Japanese conversation and struggled to fit in. Within a few months in the United States, however, we kids realized we were forgetting our Japanese. Mom and dad must have smiled wryly at this idea: their children were forgetting their "mother" tongue—Japanese—under pressure to prove that they had not "gone native." Fortunately, it took only a few days of life back in Tokyo to repair the linguistic damage.

Not that everything was paradise in Japan for young Americans, even for those who had no trouble with the Japanese language. At elementary school, Japanese kids our own age would come up behind us, pull our hair, then run off shouting "Gaijin! Gaijin!" ("Foreigner! Foreigner!") It needs to be pointed out that, however smart and well-mannered the Japanese were in comparison with typical Americans of the same age, Japanese can be, and often are, almost instinctively xenophobic. Japanese tend to have the greatest difficulty mastering foreign languages. When they travel abroad they usually prefer to travel in groups and to stay with, or at least be surrounded by, other Japanese. The word *gaijin* (foreigner) to Japanese conveys absolute "otherness," and not just the attribute of belonging to a different nationality. Sometimes the hair-pulling would develop into fist-fights, or Japanese kids would wait until they saw us in an isolated area and then they would throw rocks at us. Coached by my dad, I never stopped loving the Japanese for their many talents and qualities, but relations with Japanese children my own age were not always harmonious.

On the other hand, one of my strongest memories as a child in Japan was being approached by Japanese adults who couldn't get over how generous the United States had been to Japan after the war. Again and again, my parents, my siblings and I would be stopped in the street and told, "Thank you, thank you, America," followed by a deep bow and a hug. As kids, we didn't really understand what this meant, but the name "McArthur" would often come up. The Japanese who reached out to us with those expressions of gratitude would often also make clear that they had not objected to the American use of the atomic bomb. Given the widespread belief that the Japanese aversion to war as a means of national policy—a doctrine inscribed into the Japanese constitution—was derived chiefly from the dropping of two atomic bombs on Japan, it may surprise a few people to note that many Japanese expressed great pleasure to us youngsters that America *had* used nuclear weapons against Japan. "If it had not happened, those crazy rulers of ours would have had us fighting man to man," was one sentiment I repeatedly heard. Dropping the atomic bombs had been "the only thing that stopped the war" they would say. Even today I often pay a visit to a well-dressed elderly lady, now quite wealthy because her original home was in an extremely high-value area of Tokyo. For years she would tell me, "We rejoiced when we saw the American bombers flying across Tokyo. The bombing was terrible, but when it started happening we knew that the war was finally going to end and our nightmare would as well."

The American troops who liberated Japan were very well received. They didn't try to coerce the Japanese into changing their cultural traditions. Instead, in that naïve, innocent, almost childish way of down-home Americans suddenly transplanted into a foreign place, they made strenuous efforts to get themselves liked. In addition to the US government-supplied emergency food aid to Japan after World War II, ordinary American soldiers handed out food and chocolate to Japanese families, and especially children, they had come to know. The phrase "give me chocolate" was learned by a whole generation of people, now in their seventies and eighties who would remember it fondly, the goodness that twenty-something-year-old American kids had brought to them over half a century ago. American military engineers repaired Japanese schools and hospitals. Over the seven-year period of the occupation, they also nurtured the Japanese people into adopting a constitution that is the foundation of Japanese democracy and has ensured a near-allergy among ordinary Japanese to the use of force in settling international disputes. In fact, Article Nine of the Japanese constitution declares, "Aspiring sincerely to an international peace based on justice and order, the Japanese people forever renounce war as a sovereign right of the nation and the threat or use of force as means of settling international disputes. (2) To accomplish the aim of the preceding paragraph, land, sea, and air forces, as well as other war potential, will never be maintained. The right of belligerency of the state will not be recognized." To this day once in a while I visit a small Japanese restaurant in the Ogikubo district of Tokyo. It's a remarkable experience for an American, so many years after the war against Japan ended, because the owner comes over to my table, sits down in an empty chair there and projects a take-charge attitude. "Shut up and listen!" he says. "We owe everything to America! If America had not won the war and liberated us and rebuilt us, the Russians would have taken over and we would be like North Korea! Got it? Everything we have is because of America. Now, what was it you wanted to order?" I receive the same lecture every time. I sometimes reflect sadly that his own people, especially the twenty-somethings, needed to hear that message more than I did.

***

I have, of course, visited the United States a few times since childhood. On one trip in 1973, when I was just 16, I worked on a ship that was sailing from Yokohama to Long Beach. There I stayed with a former chaplain to Japan who was now living in California. While at his home I heard reports of a dynamic Christian church in Costa Mesa, 40 miles south of Los Angeles. It was called Calvary Chapel and had been started by someone named Chuck Smith. I was curious. Of course, having been raised in a missionary home, I could hardly have avoided making a commitment to Christ as a small boy. Indeed, this happened when I was six when another missionary boy, Donnie Hoke, a few years older than me, was knocked down and almost killed by a car. On learning he was going to live, we were all relieved as we came home from the hospital where he was being treated. But my mother used this close call with death of someone I knew well to give me a lesson in Christian doctrine. "Do you know what would have happened to you if you had died like Donnie nearly did?" she asked me. I said I didn't. Mother then explained the Christian message of salvation, and I asked the Lord into my life. I guess I must have thought I was now theologically all set to live out the rest of my childhood and youth.

Yet what happened to me at Calvary Chapel that summer of 1973 completely blew me away. There was nothing very special, or even appealing about Chuck Smith himself. To me he just seemed like any older guy with a bald head and a pot belly. He stood up at the microphone in the tent that had been erected at Costa Mesa, read a few Bible verses, and then sat down. It was the testimonies of the young people who then came up to the microphone in front of the platform that really caught my attention. They would say things like "I want to thank the Lord for helping me this week," and then provide a very down-to-earth story of what had happened to them. It seemed absolutely real to me. It wasn't a canned missionary-style message. I remember saying to myself, "For the first time I have met real Christians other than my parents. They really mean what they are saying."

I was stunned by what I was hearing and seeing. But it was on my way back to Long Beach where I was staying that something suddenly happened to me. Some presence—and I interpreted it immediately as the presence of the Lord—came upon me so powerfully that I had to get off my bicycle. I didn't really understand what was happening. I can say only that this "presence," this feeling that I was encountering holiness, was so powerful that I could no longer ride my bicycle. I put it down in a field next to the road and wept, saying over and over again, "Thank you, Jesus." I didn't know what else to do.

The visit to Calvary Chapel changed my life because, as a youth on the cusp of adulthood, I had made a very specific commitment to turn my life over to Christ. Of course, I had no real idea what that might mean for me in the future, or how it would affect my career and professional life. One direct consequence of that decision, however, and of being somewhat familiar with the Los Angeles area, was my application and acceptance at Biola University, La Mirada, California, in Los Angeles County.

My high school years had been spent at The Christian Academy in Japan, except for two years when my parents returned to the United States for their furlough and obligatory speaking in churches from which their support came. I had made many friends at the academy and in a way the whole community was an extended family of uncles, cousins, grandparents. When the time came for my departure to enroll as an undergraduate at Biola University in August 1975, it seemed that an entire tribe of relatives and friends were at the airport to see me off. Of course,

I was not new to the United States, but I was still far from comfortable there. Cars drove on the wrong side of the road, it seemed to me. You climbed onto buses entirely differently from what I was used to in Toky—in Japan we boarded from the front while in Los Angeles they boarded from the back. And people's phone numbers seemed all wrong. I kept forgetting to add the area codes to numbers. Then, of course, there was the food. This had seemed odd to me on my first trip to the US at the age of six and it was still distinctly alien.

Yet I was not the only MK (missionary kid) who was an entering undergraduate at Biola. With me all the way from Japan were three other American missionary kids who seemed as disorientated as I was. I tried from the outset at Biola to maintain dignity by being called "Ken," a regular American first name. But my three fellow MK friends from Japan once saw me unexpectedly across a room at Biola and yelled out the greeting "Kimbo," the name by which I had been known in Japan by my Japanese classmates. From then on, everyone at Biola started using the name "Kimbo" for me.

While being at a college in California was all new and exciting, each of us missed Japan so very much. The arrival of regular "care" packages of noodles, seaweed, rice crackers and other things certainly helped. We would often gather after a hard day on campus and discuss our fundamental loneliness. In many respects, we were Japanese, not American.

We sought an escape from this homesickness, a sort of alienation from Anglo-Saxon college life, by showing up at the cafeteria, making a show of eating, and then rushing quickly back to our rooms to put together a makeshift "normal" Japanese meal from our accumulated care packages.

Everything was going fine, except when it came to the point

of disposing of our leftovers after we'd finished eating. Rather than dumping the food in a trash can—which might have attracted unwelcome attention—we simply flushed the remains of the meals down the toilet. Not surprisingly, the entire plumbing of the college quickly became blocked. We returned one afternoon to our dorm rooms to discover a major new construction project under way. The maintenance people wanted to know what had clogged the campus sewage system and were tearing up the pipes to find out. When the plumbers in their autopsy of the system came across knots of rice and noodles clogging the pipes, it didn't take the college administrators long to figure out who was responsible. Biola's "Japanese Restaurant" was forced to close.

My coming to faith at Calvary Chapel two years earlier had remained a transforming experience. At Biola, it was wonderful to be able to pray, worship, and hear teaching about the Bible in English. It was at the college, however, that I found myself being drawn into deeper spiritual things; I developed a thirst for prayer and a yearning for spiritual revival on the campus. The yearning for revival had been sparked by a visit to the campus of a well-known revivalist preacher and teacher, J. Edwin Orr. He had opened my mind to what can be accomplished through prayer and revival. In response, I began a 24-hour prayer line on campus. Students could call day and night and ask for prayer. This led to a slowly growing movement to see a revival, a genuine change of heart, a genuine search for godliness, to come to the campus. Biola had been planted in the wake of the Azusa Street Pentecostal revival in Los Angeles, a turn of the century rediscovery of Pentecostalism that was to have a profound impact on the Christian church worldwide. The Pentecostal or Charismatic branch of global Christendom is believed to number upwards of 500 million adherents in every country on earth and continues to grow at a rapid rate.

I found a few students who shared my burden for revival and we began putting up posters around campus encouraging people to "Pray for Revival." We also put advertisements in major Christian magazines calling readers to "Pray for Revival and Spiritual Awakening on the Campus of Biola College." The response was overwhelming. People wrote to us from all over the world telling us that they were praying for us.

But not everyone was pleased. I was called into the office of the dean and told to stop the campaign for revival. "What on earth is wrong with praying for revival?" I asked.

"It's bad for the school's image if a group of students is running around asking for Biola to be revived. It makes us sound like a bunch of pagans instead of a Christian school that was itself founded after a Christian revival."

But I wasn't prepared to stop my campaign now that it was well under way and I had some resources at my disposal. In my first year on campus I had become the campaign manager of a student who was running for office on the student board. I did everything for the campaign: managing it, arranging meetings, putting up posters. To my great annoyance, however, after all my heavy-lifting on his behalf, he decided not to run after all. It was only days before the scheduled voting. I decided there and then to run in his place. Because of my effective organization and campaigning on his behalf, I won, and joined the student government of Biola College.

As the movement for revival gathered steam, this became an asset. I was elected chairman of the Chapel Board, a sort of student chaplain position. This gave me the authority to invite whomever I wanted to come and speak on campus. It wasn't long before I took advantage of the opportunity of inviting Chuck

Smith, the pastor of Calvary Chapel where I had experienced such a wonderful conversion experience two years before entering Biola.

Not everyone was pleased with this decision. Several people on campus were opposed to inviting a pastor so famous in Pentecostal and Charismatic circles. Perhaps they thought he'd introduce dancing in the aisles of the gymnasium or teach everyone to speak in tongues. But on the day of his appearance, he did almost exactly what I'd seen him do at Costa Mesa a few years earlier. He approached the podium matter-of-factly, opened the Bible to read several verses of scripture and then sat down. No speaking in tongues or rolling on the floor. Nothing. I suspect some of the school authorities wanting me to fail as chaplain and chief agitator for revival, were disappointed that I hadn't embarrassed myself with an emotional display on the part of my invited speaker.

Meanwhile, the few of us who were resolute to see revival come to Biola didn't stop praying or putting up posters calling on the students and faculty to pray for revival. In fact, a sort of guerrilla war got under way, with the authorities and staff pulling down posters almost as fast as we put them up. In the gymnasium itself we erected a poster too big for anyone to pull down without causing a riot. The gigantic "Pray for Revival" poster covered an entire wall of the gymnasium where the chapel services were held.

I was becoming more and more convinced in my prayers that revival would indeed come to the college. In fact, I was in a permanent state of fear that revival would come and I would miss it; I'd be away from the school or for some reason unable to attend normal chapel services. I'd be in the supermarket on the other side of the street from the gymnasium and would rush back as chapel time approached, my heart almost missing a beat in case today was the day for revival to come and I would not be present to witness it. But I always found, of course, that things were proceeding normally in the chapel and my fears had been groundless.

I must have seemed a fanatic to some people. I'd often spend the night before the main chapel service of the week in prayer. I'd pray over every seat in the gymnasium, begging God to bring revival the next day. Sometimes before the start of the chapel service some friends and I would drive around the main campus seven times—a sort of Joshua-at-Jericho movement—in prayer for the college and all of the students, staff, and faculty who would be attending the chapel service.

One of the top news stories in 1977 was the return to the United States and conversion of former Black Panther Eldridge Cleaver. Escaping charges for murder resulting from a gun fight, Eldridge had left the US, traveling the world with his family in an attempt to find the perfect Marxist country. First he went to Cuba where his first child, Maceo, was born and named by Fidel Castro. Rather than a Marxist paradise, however, he found instead racism and discrimination. Disenchanted, he next went to North Korea where he was welcomed by Kim Ill Sun. His second child was named by the leader, Joju. As time passed, Eldridge once again became disenchanted, this time by the nightmarish police state to which North Koreans were subjected. Eldridge, at the end of his rope, eventually found his way to Paris where one night as he looked up at the sky he saw the faces of his heroes pass one by one across the face of the moon: Marx, Fidel Castro, and then finally one face stopped. It was the face of Jesus. Eldridge found himself quietly singing a song his mother had taught him when he was a child—"Jesus loves all the children..." That night, looking up to the sky with tears in his eyes, Eldridge came home to his faith. The next day he called the US Embassy and made arrangements to return to Oakland, California, and face charges.

After working very hard, we arranged for Eldridge to speak at Biola in October of 1977. Due to bad weather at the Orange County Airport, however, his plane was not able to land. While waiting at the airport to pick him up, we sent word back to Biola about the situation and asked those at the chapel service to pray. Suddenly, out of the clouds, the plane landed. When we got to the chapel, everyone in attendance had bowed heads in prayer for Eldridge. Those prayers had opened a hole in the clouds, and Eldridge himself felt it had been a miracle. In what he called "one of the best days of my life," which he inscribed in the front of my Bible, Eldridge walked into the electric presence of the Biola gymnasium and told his story of finding Christ.

The presence of God was heavy in the room that day, and students were permanently touched. Following his visit, I kept in touch with Eldridge and knew of the breakup of his marriage. When his wife, Kathleen, was offered a position at Yale University, I met with her to ask if she would return to Eldridge. As so often happens, Eldridge was a revolutionary but not a good person for day-to-day life. Kathleen who had stood by him during all the terrible times was tired and wanted to pursue her own dreams.

Eldridge settled in Oakland, and I regularly visited him doing what I could to help him rebuild his new life. The last time I saw him, he was sitting on the sofa in his living room, smiling that sweet, sad and always hopeful smile that so many loved.

And then it happened. The revival came on an October day in 1980.

As soon as I entered the gymnasium, I realized something was different. As I made my way to my regular seat at the front of the bleachers another student stopped me and whispered in my ear. He told me that one of the most popular students on campus, Tobin Sorensen, had died in an accident the previous day. Tobin was an athlete, a keen rock-climber and a warm, outgoing personality. But he was really most famous because he was such a zealous Christian who loved nothing more than to share his faith as often as he could and to encourage other believers to be zealous too.

Perhaps Tobin's death was the jolt that both I and Biola had been needing. I knew that, as student chaplain, I had to be the one to break the news to the students and faculty assembled in the gymnasium. I walked up to the microphone and made the announcement of Tobin's death. The silence that followed was deafening. I went on, "His death touches us all. He was the one person on this camps always talking about the Lord, encouraging us to give our lives to Him." I paused. "I need to repent," I said. Barely aware of what I was doing, for I hadn't planned any of this in advance, I walked to the front of the podium from which speakers address the auditorium and knelt down, asking others who felt so inclined to join me.

At first there was just silence as I knelt there completely alone in front of some 2,000 students, faculty, and staff. Then, beginning slowly as a quiet shuffling, rising to a noisy roar as more and more people joined in, hundreds of students and professors joined me on the floor, kneeling in repentance for sins they felt they had committed against each other. Students approached professors and confessed incidents of cheating, professors asked forgiveness of students for having ignored them or treated them arrogantly. Everyone, it seemed, had committed some grievance against another for which he or she wanted forgiveness.

What followed for several days was an amazing and quite

wonderful time of peace, forgiveness, reconciliation, and renewal of faith. Nobody who was touched by this experience could forget it. Many people's lives were changed permanently.

We decided that what had begun at Biola should infect as many other campuses as we could reach, so student teams were formed to go out and spread the news. My vision from the Lord, which had come to me through the lecturing of J. Edwin Orr, was simple: Prayer, Revival and Mission. Prayer was always the foundation for revival, but revival would motivate new generations of young people to go out into the mission field.

Many of us who had caught the fire of revival at Biola went on to attend "Edinburgh 80", an event designed to focus on missionary efforts that was held on the one hundredth anniversary of the 19th Century Edinburgh Student Missions Teams. Several of us also attended, as a group, the Urbana Conference 1980, an annual, mission-focused gathering organized by InterVarsity Christian Fellowship and held every four years during the month of January in Urbana, Illinois. It was at Urbana that the National Student Missions Conference had begun, and it was at Urbana that the organization Theological Students for Frontier Missions was established. We Biolans organized ourselves into teams and visited campuses all over California and other states trying to spread the message of revival and galvanize fellow students for mission work. As a result of this extensive canvassing and through the work of the National Student Missions Consultation, TSFM, and the Caleb Foundation, thousands of young people were called to the Mission Field. Amazingly, 20 years later when I was in Los Angeles for a short visit, it happened again. A student stood up in a chapel and shouted out, "God can do it again" and asked for forgiveness for something he had done. In the days that followed, lines of students—just as they had done

20 years earlier—lined up to throw away items they felt they no longer needed and asked for forgiveness. The blessing of God flowed once again. Just as J. Edwin Orr had said nearly a quarter century before, revival was the way God renewed His people. Orr's research had shown that the direct results of the First and Second Great Awakenings to hit the United States had resulted in economic revival as well as spiritual, and had delayed the economic depression by a generation.

As is often the case either preceding or following great spiritual breakthroughs, however, I found myself subjected to a monsoon of discouragement, even depression. The high-pressure job of being the college chaplain at a time of spiritual awakening on campus was intense and difficult. Looking back, I can see that I was the front-line target of spiritual warfare, a condition all serious Christians recognize as an effort by the Adversary to get us down in the dumps and hinder us from what we were sure was God's work in our lives. I became discouraged about life in general to the point of depression. I felt I had somehow failed God. At the end of my rope, and determined to fast and pray until I got an answer from God, I borrowed a small cabin near Santa Rosa, California, where I had visited earlier while modeling clothes for a Japanese TV commercial. Fasting—the deliberate self-denial of food and sometimes life's little luxuries—is a time-honored tradition among Christians of all denominational traditions to get closer to God and to be attentive to what He seems to be saying.

One of the books I happened to take along for this sojourn in solitude was a book called *Yes, Lord*, by Harald Bredesen. I didn't know who he was and soon afterwards discovered that he was almost a legend in Christian circles. Deeply impressed by the book, above all for the examples in it of Bredesen's experiences of radical obedience to divine leading, I hunted around and managed to find a phone number for Harald. He was living in Escondido, California. Not quite sure what response I would get—I'd probably be talking to the third assistant secretary to the assistant flunkey—I nearly dropped the receiver when the phone was answered by none other than Harald Bredesen himself. "I've just read your book and am at the end of my rope," I blurted out. "Can I talk to you?"

Instead of quoting scripture or offering soothing pastoral advice over the phone, Bredesen simply responded, "Why don't you come down and stay with us for a while?"

That was an invitation I accepted with alacrity, driving the 70 miles south from Los Angeles to Escondido where Harald lived. Harald was waiting for me in the driveway of his simple, ranch-style home and quickly introduced me to his equally welcoming wife, Gen, and their children. Harald "sentenced" me, as quid pro quo for learning from him, to take charge of his vegetable garden.

It was the perfect therapy for a burned out student. Far away from the city in the Bredesens' wonderful country home, I was nursed back to health and sanity. I earned my keep by taking care of Harald and Gen's vegetable garden. Every day as I watched the vegetables first taking firm root in the soil and then steadily rising up from it, I found myself naturally and unselfconsciously replanting my own spiritual roots. Harald and Gen Bredesen became my home away from home, my adoptive spiritual family. I worked for Harald Bredesen for many years as his secretary after that, reading and reviewing and writing letters for him, traveling with him to speaking engagements across the country. Harald had long been something of a legend in Christian evangelical circles. He had led countless people to Christ, and many Christians into a new experience with the Holy Spirit. In my many phone conversations with people who wanted to contact him, I found myself often wondering if the person I happened to be speaking to at that moment was going through the same discouragement I had encountered, and was perhaps "at the end of his rope."

***

The year was 1979 and tumultuous events had taken place in the Middle East. President Jimmy Carter in September 1978 had brokered a path-breaking peace agreement between Israel and Egypt after intense negotiations at Camp David. Yet a few months later the Shah of Iran, for many years a staunch ally of the US, had been overthrown by followers of the Ayatollah Khomeini, a fanatical Shiite cleric who had come to power after his followers in Iran had staged a revolution against the Shah.

Interestingly, Harald Bredesen had a close relationship with Egyptian President Anwar Sadat, after initially interviewing him for ABC News. Indeed, Bredesen had written the prayer which had been read at the beginning of the Camp David negotiations. Bredesen had such a remarkable manner of getting to know prominent people and leaders and then speaking to them in persuasive terms about his Christian faith that former *New York Times* editor Bob Slosser described him as "minister to world leaders."

One day at Biola I received a phone call from Harald. As usual, he didn't waste time on small talk. "I need you to come with me to Egypt to pray for Anwar Sadad," he blurted out. "But I am in the middle of exams," I protested. "Anyway, how on earth am I going to get the money I need for a ticket to Egypt?"

"The Lord will provide," said Harald, in his inimitable, child-like way.

I didn't doubt Harald's own faith, but I seriously doubted the professors and authorities at Biola would consent to my sudden absence from school. I had already caused immense trouble to the school administration by my various antics, not excluding my disruption of the school sewage system during my first year at the college. I was reluctant to give my real reason for wanting to go to Egypt—"to pray for Sadat" as Harald had put it—because it surely sounded too unbelievable to down-to-earth college professors. I immediately went to my various teachers to try and get out of class, knowing that they would all say "no" because they were familiar with my reputation for being disruptive at Biola. I didn't want to give the real reason for my forthcoming travels as they would never have believed me, but I was finally forced to say that I was going on a trip to pray for the president of Egypt, Anwar Sadat, and for the terminally ill and recently exiled Shah of Iran, who had been allowed into Egypt after rather shabby treatment by the US and some of its allies. Needless to say, my professors were not especially impressed by this name-dropping. Several of them flatly refused to excuse my absence from their classes. Yet others did respond gracefully, and with a measure of their own faith. "Go ahead," they said, "and don't worry about exams. We will work something out."

Harald liked to do a lot of things on the fly, including buying his airline tickets for overseas travel or planning any itinerary at all. I was supposed to meet Harald at Los Angeles International Airport, and there—somehow or other—there were supposed to be tickets to Egypt for both of us. I spotted him quickly, and we made our way to the Japan Airlines counter. We had decided that the best itinerary was to fly Japan Airlines first to Tokyo, and then across Asia to Cairo.

But—I should have anticipated this, knowing Harald as well as I did—neither he nor I had tickets to board the plane. Harald didn't show the slightest degree of fluster. "The Lord will provide," he said—I thought rather smugly—and we simply stood by the Japan Airlines check-in counter as though it was the most natural thing in the world to plan an air trip across the Pacific Ocean and most of the Continent of Asia without the remotest visible possibility of paying for the tickets. As we stood close to the check-in counter, however, a wealthy-looking man who was a complete stranger to me, but who obviously knew Harald, came up to both of us, withdrew a checkbook from the inside pocket of his coat and paid for the tickets. I was flabbergasted, but Harald seemed to think it the most natural thing in the world.

The flight, of course, stopped in Tokyo, and I was able to visit my surprised family. Harald made a quick side-trip to Seoul, Korea, where he visited Dr. Paul Yonggi Cho, pastor of Full Gospel Central Church, a mega church that even then had a membership of more than 100,000 members. After Harald's visit, hundreds of thousands of Koreans in Dr. Cho's church started praying for an open door in Egypt for two Americans who were on their way to pray for the Egyptian president and the exiled Shah of Iran. Our flight had actually been divided into two parts: first to Tokyo from Los Angeles, and then from Tokyo to Cairo. But the second part of the trip had been arranged in such haste that we were not aware before we took off from Narita Airport and began chatting to the Japan Airlines cabin crew that we were going to make a technical stop for refueling in Tehran.

It was like being hit by a glassful of ice water. In July 1980, the time of our trip, 52 American hostages were still being held in the US embassy building in the Iranian capital. They had been taken prisoner there in November 1979 when angry Iranian militants swarmed over the walls of the American embassy and initiated a captivity of diplomats and staffers that was to last 444 days. To land at Tehran Airport presented certainly no problem for the Japanese passengers aboard the aircraft; the Iranians bore no grudges against the Japanese. But who knew how the Revolutionary Guards would respond if they boarded the plane and found two additional Americans had landed in Iran?

I immediately woke Harald who was fast asleep in the seat next to me. Earlier in the flight he had been excitedly talking to the passengers around us, explaining the Gospel as he always did, and explaining loudly that we were both on our way to pray for the President of Egypt and the Shah of Iran. He laughed when he heard the news, as he often did when someone told him of an up-coming problem. "Don't worry," he said in a voice full of assurance that I certainly did not feel. "Everything will be okay." Even before we landed at Tehran, Harold fell back to sleep.

It wasn't okay. Some 40 minutes had passed since our touchdown for refueling, and that process had already been completed. Why were we still on the ground? Suddenly a group of Revolutionary Guards burst brusquely onto the plane and demanded to see everyone's passports. I noticed that the Japan Airlines flight attendants were having an intense discussion among themselves in Japanese. They were all wearing worried expressions. Finally, one of them made his way quietly to where Harald and I were sitting in the back half of the aircraft. The Revolutionary Guards were taking their time methodically scrutinizing all the Japanese passports. "Quickly," hissed the flight attendant, "take your friend to the back of the plane and try to hide." I awoke Harald again and half-carried him as far back as there were still rows of seats on the aircraft I actually set him down on the floor of the plane behind the last row of seats. "Don't worry, don't worry," he kept mumbling. "Everything will be all right." He promptly fell asleep again. I crouched down beside him, trying to be as inconspicuous as possible.

I waited in horror as the Revolutionary Guards made their way towards where we were, examining every passport they took from all the passengers. What saved us from arrest or worse was a brave Japanese flight attendant—the one who had warned me in the first place—who insisted to the Iranians that there was no one else on the plane to account for. The Revolutionary Guards shrugged disdainfully and exited the plane. What had been anticipated as a 40-minute stopover turned into two hours of terrifying suspense. Everyone, including the Japanese crew, heaved a sigh of relief after the Revolutionary Guards left. When the plane finally took off to resume its journey, Harald was still asleep. Knowing how loud and talkative he could be when he was excited about something, I was relieved.

After we landed at Cairo airport we were taken by an Egyptian government car to the hotel where we were to stay. The next day, we were driven to Ismailia, at the northern end of the Suez Canal, where we were scheduled to meet with President Sadat of Egypt. Ever since Harald had conducted an interview on ABC with Sadat, he would often be requested by the Egyptian embassy, in particular Mohammed Hakki in Washington, to pray with Sadat by phone. Sadat certainly didn't avow himself to be a Christian in any conventional way. Indeed, his frequent mosque attendance had led to the formation of a bump on his forehead where he allowed his forehead to strike the ground in prostrating himself as part of the Islamic worship service. Yet there was something about him that Christians might ordinarily call "godly." Western journalists sometimes called him "mystical" because of his tendency, when preparing for a major decision, to retire into solitude, even reclusiveness, for his reflections. He would often go to the desert for days at a time just simply to pray. At such a time not even his wife or any of his other family members were allowed to have communication with him.

Sadat's early career had been a dramatic one. Though educated at Egyptian military schools run by the British who controlled Egypt for the first half of the twentieth century, Sadat had sympathized with the Germans during World War II, as Rommel's forces were pushing back the British from Tripoli in Libya to Egypt itself. He was arrested by the British on suspicion of spying for the Germans, and held in prison. There he was permitted to read politically "safe" books in Arabic translation. One that he devoured while in prison and which seemed to have an electrifying effect on him was *The Robe*, a 1942 historical novel about the Crucifixion written by Lloyd C. Douglas. The book was one of the best-selling titles of the 1940's, rising to the top of the *New York Times* best-seller list in November 1942, four weeks after first getting onto the list. It held the position for nearly a year. In 1953 a movie version of the novel was released. Sadat seems to have been profoundly moved after reading *The Robe* in his British prison cell in Egypt. Years later, after he had become president of Egypt in 1970, following the death of his predecessor Gamel Abdul Nasser, one of his childhood friends and now a leading imam in Egypt, came to him for help. The imam's daughter had been attending a school in Belgium and was unexpectedly diagnosed with cancer. Two Catholic nuns who visited the hospital in Brussels where she was being treated had prayed over her and she had apparently been healed of the cancer. She had then quickly phoned up her father in Egypt, the imam, and blurted out over the phone, "Jesus healed me." It was a brave—or foolhardy—thing for the daughter of Egypt's leading Islamic cleric to say. But instead of promptly disowning his daughter, the imam astonished her by saying, "I know. He was just in my room." The Egyptian cleric himself had experienced a visionary encounter, which he was sure was with Jesus himself.

That, however, was not something any ordinary Egyptian, let alone an imam, could speak of openly in Egypt without putting his own life in immediate danger. He visited his friend President Sadat and narrated the story to him. Sadat, as he explained later to Harald Bredesen, immediately reassured the cleric. He said, "We both know what we have always talked about—our searching for God. This is truly God." Sadat ensured the cleric's safe departure from Egypt for refuge overseas.

On arrival at Sadat's country estate in Ismailia, Harald and I found him surrounded by a large contingent of security agents. After greeting us warmly he looked in the direction of his guards and sighed. "I keep telling the security guys to leave me alone," he said. "They insist I wear a bullet-proof vest and have them all around me all the time, but it is my belief that God has given me a job to do. Until that job is finished nobody will ever be able to hurt me. When the job is finished nobody will be able to protect me."

We were deeply touched by this. Sadat in some hard-to-define way was a man of God. Harald and I had the distinct impression that he knew Christ in the same way that we did and that he was a fellow believer. I knew about his retreating into the desert to fast and pray for hours before major decisions. At his residence in Ismailia we spent hours talking and praying with him as he opened up from his heart about his country, his faith and finally, about the Shah of Iran, who was then his guest in Egypt.

"In the past you came to pray with me," he told us. "This time I need you to pray for the Shah. He is deeply depressed and needs a miracle from God."

A few hours later we took our leave of this wonderful Egyptian leader with many prayers and hugs. We prayed that God would bless him, protect him, and continue to use him. I asked him to sign my Bible, and there is still his distinct signature in it with the date, "July 6, 1980."

It was the last time we saw him. Fifteen months later, while attending a military parade outside Cairo on the eighth anniversary of the beginning of the Yom Kippur War of 1973 (which the Egyptians call the October War), Sadat was gunned down by a fanatical young army officer who was part of a small conspiratorial group of Egyptian Islamists. When I learned that at the time of the assassination Vice-President Mubarak, who was sitting beside him and who succeeded him, had tried to pull him down as the assassins ran towards the presidential reviewing stand, I smiled. Sadat had faced death like a man, standing up to face the bullets in the conviction that God himself would stop them if he still had divine tasks to perform and that, if his time had come to an end, there would be nothing he could do to stave off death.

From Ismailia, we were driven to another of Sadat's palaces, this time in Cairo, the one which he had lent to his friend, the Shah of Iran. It was a large, stately mansion in one of Cairo's best neighborhoods.

We knew before arriving that the Shah was bedridden, and indeed was probably in the last few weeks of his life. It was thus no surprise that we were greeted at the door of the residence by the Shah's chamberlain, his beautiful wife, Farah Pahlavi (who also signed my Bible with the inscription, "Thank you for praying for us. Farah Pahlavi, Cairo, July 6, 1980") and taken immediately into his bedroom. There we saw the Shah in his bed propped up by pillows.

As we walked in he suddenly sat up. "Who is it?" he cried. His wife rushed to his side and said, "We have visitors."

He replied "No, it is not them," he said. "There is a presence—it has entered the room." Harald and I looked at each other but said nothing. Then Harald sat down in a chair that had been brought to the Shah's bedside. "Your majesty," he began, "what you sensed just now was the presence of Jesus, whom we brought here with us. Then a young woman who had joined our group in Cairo, the wife of Richard Freds, son of the late Oral Freds who founded Oral Freds University, began signing some Christian choruses for the Shah. He lay there with tears flowing down both his cheeks. Then he poured out his heart to us, as if wanting us to know how pained he was on behalf of the people of Iran.

"You know, I spent my life as Shah trying to bring my people out of poverty. I wanted to make Iran a great, first-world nation. I wanted to do this in my lifetime. I should have been more careful, I should not have listened to all my advisors. I thought my people really loved me until the one day when I looked outside the window and saw them demonstrating against me." He dissolved into tears and sobbing as his wife sat next to him on the other side of the bed."

You know," Harald responded, "God has been with you all along, working out his plan for you and the people of Iran." Ever the evangelist, Harald then asked the Shah if he would like to pray to receive Christ. The Shah prayed together with Harold. The "presence" that he seemed to have noticed when Harald and I entered the room appeared to have calmed his spirit. Days later, he asked that the medication and treatment he was receiving for his lymphatic cancer be stopped. He seemed to think that, after his death, the resentment at America for having allowed the Shah into the United States for medical treatment would come to an end and the hostages being held in the US embassy in Tehran would be allowed to go home. It was a profoundly generous impulse. How many of us would offer to have our medical treatment suspended if there was hope of staving off death for a few days or weeks? But that is what the Shah of Iran did on his deathbed. For all of his faults, he was a man who truly loved his country, and in the end, gave his life in a dramatic contrast to those who rule Iran today.

CHAPTER THREE

DORM ROOM ANTICS

DAYS LATER, I was back at Biola telling the story of what had happened to the professors who had approved my absence and trying to placate the others who had been irritated that I would not be able to sit through their exams. Though the excitement of the revival and its follow-up remained on the campus, I had, quite independent of that, begun to work from my Biola base within weeks of arriving on campus in September of 1975. My MK friends and I had started receiving phone calls from Japanese we did not know but who somehow knew about me and my MK friends. A typical conversation would begin with a complete stranger saying, "We are friends of your friends from the bicycle shop in your neighborhood of Tokyo," or something like that. Basically some of the Japanese we knew had passed on my phone number to *their* friends.

All of the callers had some kind of problem. They had lost their luggage at the airport, or had gotten involved in a car-wreck, or found out that the hotel where they had made a room reservation was over-booked. All the problems were typical travelers' problems and didn't really require a brain surgeon to solve—just someone who spoke Japanese and understood Japanese society. From our various small dorm rooms at Biola we did what we could. Sometimes this meant providing accommodation for a stranger—and otherwise homeless—Japanese student who had found out from a phone conversation where Biola University was. It wasn't long before a Japanese student or two would be discovered taking a shower in the bathrooms of our dormitory. Inevitably, we got reported on by fellow-students irritated that their living-space and bathroom facilities had suddenly been invaded by people *they* didn't know, and Japanese people, at that. We had to find accommodation for the visitors on an off-campus site.

The calls continued coming. One day, I received our first call from a Japanese traveler who was not in Los Angeles, but some other city. I think it was Chicago. We were non-plussed. We ourselves couldn't do anything for a Chicago-located Japanese traveler from where we were living in Los Angeles. We called around and then remembered that one of the Japanese with whom I had gone to school in Tokyo was studying at a university in Chicago. I called him up and asked if he could help this Japanese stranger who had contacted us. With this experience, we built up a notebook of names, addresses and phone numbers of people in American cities who could be called upon to help meet the needs of Japanese in distress.

We had decided to call our visiting Japanese rescue organization—if it could be called an organization—Agape House. The word *agape* is from the Greek text of the New Testament. The apostle Paul often used it to denote selfless, giving love quite unconnected with family love, which is often called "filial," or romantic love between a man and a woman. Gradually, word about Agape House spread to different parts of Japan, and we were almost inundated with requests for help from beleaguered Japanese travelers trying to cope with the complexity of modern America just as we had encountered it years earlier. Sooner or later, I was sure, the Japanese press would pick up the story, and when they did, our operation would surely move altogether to another level.

It happened sooner rather than later. The Japanese daily newspaper, *Asahi Shimbun*, had obtained my phone number from one of the many Japanese we had helped out. *Asahi* has a daily readership in Japan of 21 million people, so we should have known that, after agreeing to be interviewed by phone, we would be totally deluged by Japanese travelers with problems. The article on Agape House and the informal hotline for Japanese travelers in the US ran in the newspaper. The fall-out was instant. Suddenly we began to get calls from Japanese all over the United States. We received our first international enquiry in the form of a letter from a Japanese student in London having trouble at school.

Unsolicited donations also began coming in from unknown Japanese who had been touched by reading about what we were doing. From a modest California dorm room, Agape House had blossomed into a world-wide non-profit organization.

One spring morning in 1987 I took a call at Agape House from Japan. It was the national TV network, NHK, and they wanted to produce a news story on us. They had read the article in the *Asahi* newspaper and asked if they could come and interview us. In high school, I had worked as a model, and at college I supported myself through modeling gigs during the summer vacation. I had run into several Japanese reporters while doing this, and now they all suddenly seemed to want to resume contact.

I was by now wary of the pitfalls of unexpected publicity and turned everyone down. But, like all good journalists, they were persistent, and called me up at 4.00 a.m. every day requesting our permission to come to Los Angeles and film us. I had actually taken to waking up at 4.00 a.m. for my daily devotions, so their timing was quite good. After a few days of awakening from sleep, beginning my prayer-time, and then getting interrupted by the call from NHK, I relented.

A camera crew, producer, and reporter arrived a few days later and spent nearly three weeks filming our work. I and the others working with me bonded with them in a way that was to change the direction of my ministry, though I didn't realize it at the time. Just before it was time for the crew to fly back to Tokyo the director asked me if I would like to return to Japan with them. I would have a chance to see my family again.

I had resisted going back to Japan since arriving to study at Biola. My dad would regularly write me letters telling me to "come home." (This, of course, was long before the days of email and text-messaging.) I always justified my refusal by saying that I was doing a more powerful thing by helping Japanese in Los Angeles than anything I could possibly do in Japan. But I pondered the invitation of the NHK director as the day of his departure approached. I also prayed about his offer and got a nasty shock when, in prayer one morning, I sensed that God might actually be saying something rather directly to me: "This is your last chance," I thought I heard God very specifically nudging me. Then came the words—in my mind, or course, not audibly—"If you are not on that plane, then you can forget about going back to Japan. This is your last chance."

I was seized with fear. Did God really have specific time deadlines? If I didn't obey the command to return to Japan, would I miss some important opportunity in my life? I didn't waste any time trying to second-guess divine planning. I was on that plane with the NHK crew as soon as they decided to leave. I had been twelve years in the US. It was time to return home.

On arriving back in Tokyo I scurried around trying as quickly as possible to readjust to life at home and back in Japan; after all, it was my first home. Two days after I returned, on August 17, 1987, the NHK documentary on Agape House was aired. They called it "A summer at Agape House," and its audience was huge. Millions of Japanese viewed it, in the same way that millions of Americans would have viewed something on "Sixty Minutes," the CBS Sunday-night documentary program. Yet I didn't even watch the program and didn't think it was a big deal at all. Little did I understand its effect on the Japanese audience. The response of the public was a tsunami of letters and phone calls from all over Japan unprecedented in the history of the network. The resulting incoming calls following "A summer at Agape House" were more numerous than any previous program in the history of the network.

With my blithe inattention to the program, I was completely unaware of all this. I only began to realize something was happening when the telephone started to ring off the hook. Once I got into a taxi and the driver turned round and looked directly at me. "Ken San," he said, "you don't need to pay. Thank you for all that you have done for Japan. Where can I take you?" I was starting to realize that the program had accomplished more than I thought; even Tokyo cab drivers were giving me free trips!

What had happened was that the program had shown us reaching out to help Japanese 24/7. The entire country was touched. We became instant national heroes. I had known nothing of this. All of a sudden invitations poured in to speak, appear on TV, write books, join boards It was all becoming quite crazy.

We had started Agape House in Los Angeles. Now we began one in Japan itself and the work became something I had always prayed about; it was supported 100 percent by the Japanese. What had started as just one person—me—helped by two MK's in Los Angeles, now became a team of friends and new volunteers. We were treated as celebrities and followed everywhere. The NHK program filmed in Los Angeles was re-aired two more times. No other program had ever been aired more than twice and the program received the highest rating since Japan had started keeping track of TV show ratings. There were so many calls coming into NHK that the main phone line into the organization became overloaded and shut down. NHK had to install a special line just to accommodate calls to enquire about Agape House.

***

The Work of Agape House continued and expanded. We developed a 24-hour hotline for the international community living in Japan called the Japan Helpline in addition to the service we were providing for Japanese overseas. One day I received an invitation to speak at Chuo University, a private college in suburban Tokyo. It was an overcast day with nothing otherwise memorable about it. Two years had now passed since the Agape House had burst onto the Japanese scene.

Things had also calmed down from the frenetic pitch of activity that had followed the NHK program. I was exhausted and had become discouraged by the tedious routine of keeping going an organization whose premise was to help Japanese everywhere and foreigners in Japan in situations where no one else seemed to be helping. It happened, though, that the 1989 San Francisco earthquake had just struck the previous day—October 17, and it now dominated the news. But as I sat on the stage in a solemn-looking line of officials from the Chuo University awaiting my turn to speak, a rather crazy idea flew into my mind and perched there. I wondered if there might be any students sufficiently stirred up by my talk to volunteer to help with the consequences of the earthquake in San Francisco. I turned to one of the officials sitting near me before it was my turn and whispered the question whether I could mention the idea after my formal remarks had come to an end. "Ken San," he replied. "You just don't know our students! They are all selfish and don't care about anyone except themselves. If you ask them if any of them are willing to consider going to San Francisco, nobody will respond. Don't waste your time!" I began arguing with him, becoming increasingly angry and frustrated about the way the college seemed to be looking down on its own students. The Japanese are usually excruciatingly polite when they say no. But the official I was whispering to made it abundantly clear that the answer to my request could be understood in any language: "No, no, and again no."

I found this attitude infuriating. How could college officials be so contemptuous of their own students? Finally, it came my turn to give my talk and I rose to deliver it. There was nothing controversial in it. I delivered my by now familiar lecture in Japanese about Japan being a "special country" that ordinary Japanese and especially students needed to honor. I told the students what I and many others really appreciated about Japan. I also spoke of family, freedom, peace, and other themes that Japanese loved to hear discussed. But at the end of my formal remarks I paused, looked into the audience of eager student faces, and then blurted out, "Remember the earthquake that took place yesterday in San Francisco? How many of you would like to go to San Francisco and help out?" Immediately, twenty students raised their hands. As I watched the hands going up, the university officials came on stage and demanded that I end my lecture.

"Why?" I asked.

"You promised you would not ask the students to respond! Stop the lecture immediately! Tell the students they should not go!" They were enraged. I immediately told the kids to put their hands down. The officials were just getting warmed up.

"Even if you have a team that wants to go, you will have to pay your own way," they said. "When you get there the weather will probably be very bad—it is San Francisco." Actually, San Francisco in October is probably the loveliest time of year.

"You will most likely sleep in sleeping bags in tents and it will be wet and cold. Your work will consist of sorting and handing out emergency supplies, or feeding and taking care of those in the shelters from the earthquake. Now"—I detected a glimmer of surrender—"if you absolutely insist on proceeding with this insane idea, you can do the talking outside the lecture hall." Then, with a look that seemed to say, "That ought to fix him," they gathered up the skirts of their dignity and swept out.

To my utter surprise, when I finally made my way to the outside entrance of the lecture hall, there were no fewer than 38 students awaiting me for instructions. The original 22 who had raised their hands had almost doubled in number.

The university officials were incensed at this response by their students. "Get out! Get out immediately!" was what they shouted at me in a most un-Japanese way. I left the campus, leaving simply my phone contact number with all the students. One by one, those who had expressed interest in the proposal to go to San Francisco were contacted by the school and told that if they participated in this hare-brained scheme they would be expelled.

But the students, despite these threats, were adamant that they wanted to go.

Meanwhile, I began to wonder if I had bitten off more than I could chew. I didn't know anyone in San Francisco who could be a liaison on the ground when we arrived there. Scratching my head for ideas, I decided to call up the Salvation Army for assistance. They responded immediately to my project, and kindly agreed to pick everybody up at the airport when the group arrived and to take them to one of the sites where they were working. Japan Air Lines, Japan's national carrier, agreed to provide specially discounted tickets for the students.But the volunteers still needed both Japanese passports and US visas before they could leave Japan and enter the US. When they went to Japan's Foreign Ministry to acquire their passports, the students were told that it would take weeks to obtain them. But then something miraculous seemed to occur. At Agape House two days later I received a phone call from a downtown hotel. Former president Ronald Reagan was in town and had read about the appeal to the Japanese students, and their response, in an English-language Japanese newspaper.

The former president, out of office less than a year, wanted to meet with all the students. Within a matter of hours he had shaken hands with each one and said that he completely supported their quest to help San Francisco. This news somehow galvanized the Japanese Foreign Ministry, which now inexplicably discovered that it could issue passports in a matter of hours rather than days. The US embassy in Tokyo also absorbed the message that this entire operation was good publicity for the US and they quickly provided US entry visas for the students. The whole thing was a lesson in instant diplomacy for both them and me.

The Japan Air Lines discounted tickets hot in our hands, our group boarded a flight to San Francisco within five days of my original speech at Chuo University. Meanwhile, the Japanese media had also jumped on the story. The major daily newspaper, *Asahi Shimbun*, ran an editorial commending the students and making the case that the students were doing what the Japanese government itself should be doing. All Japanese, the editorial said, should be proud of what the students had set out to do.

Our team arrived in San Francisco and was driven by the Salvation Army from the airport to the town of Watsonville. There the students worked with the Salvation Army sorting and delivering supplies to those made homeless by the earthquake. They helped feed and clothe the refugees. There was intense media coverage in Japan and the students found themselves national celebrities. When they returned to Tokyo two weeks later they were all invited to the Foreign Ministry to explain how they had been able to accomplish such a project. The students burst out laughing. "It was easy," they told the serious-faced Japanese diplomatic mandarins. "We just contacted the Salvation Army and said we wanted to help and we went." Our team had been actually the first Japanese disaster relief team in history to travel outside the borders of Japan. Not long afterwards the Japanese government itself created a disaster team in preparedness for disasters that might arise in the future.

Finally, Chuo University decided it ought to chime in with congratulations. I received an urgent call at Agape House from the president of the college. He wanted to present the students with a special award for heroism. But they all gave him a stiff response. "When we were preparing to go," they said, "you opposed us and threatened to expel us. When we got some good publicity you all of a sudden changed. We will not accept your award." The president was as furious at this response as he had been when I had first asked the Chuo students if they wanted to go to San Francisco.

The San Francisco relief team that Agape House organized was the first of many teams we sent out, a total of 83, in fact. Since our modest beginnings in a dorm at Biola, the teams have gone to nearly every major natural disaster throughout the world, from earthquakes in Egypt, Iran, and Pakistan to typhoons and tsunamis in Indonesia and Taiwan. More recently, the team was the first to arrive at the earthquake and tsunami site in northern Japan on March 11, 2011, where it brought in Japan's only disaster relief vehicle. Our team worked to bring in disaster supplies, and then to dig out the mud left from the tsunami that devastated the area, and continues to work with the tens of thousands who are still unable to return home. One of the untold stories of the Japanese tsunami was the fact that over 24,000 American military and a nearly equal amount of Americans from throughout the world came to help Japan at their time of need. This is a story that cannot be verified, but months later, at one of the temporary housing facilities, an old man told me an amazing story.

"For the first week to ten days," he said "nobody came to help up. Except for the Americans. Twenty-four hours a day, they ran helicopters, bringing everybody from the shoreline to higher ground. When we landed, they read us a message in Japanese, which said, "Please do not tell anyone that we have helped you like this." The Americans did not want to do anything that would make the host country look bad. Wherever we went, we kept coming across the same young men and women. Many of them had just gotten back from service in Iraq or Afghanistan. The angels had moved on from Iraq to Afghanistan, and now those same young men and women were here in northern Japan, helping out with the earthquake and tsunami. Whereas before they would say they were "there to help Aye-rackies," now they were here to help the "Japaneese." From airlifting supplies to rescuing people to rebuilding schools, they were doing just the things that they had been doing in Iraq. We tried to find the American headquarters for what was called "Operation Tomodachi," or "Operation Friend" in English. We were directed to go to what used to be known as "Camp Sendai," a former American base nearby. Directed to the headquarters building, we still couldn't find the operational headquarters for the American project in the area. Finally, we found a series of desks in the hallway of the Japanese headquarters. "Is this the American headquarters?" we asked. With the same optimistic and upbeat look on their faces that we had seen in Iraq so many times, the workers responded "Yep!Yes it is!" Shocked at the fact that these angels didn't even have an office, I became very angry. "No," they said. "We're just happy that they let us help," was the answer of the commander in charge. The Japanese hadn't even provided them with an office space but it didn't matter. They were just happy to help out.

We went over to pick up some suppies which were stored in the room where they were sleeping. Despite the fact that this had been a former American base with dormitories, showers, and other facilities, the Americans were sleeping on their own cots, eating their own MREs. It made me furious. But they said, "Please don't say anything. We're just happy that they let us help out." It was the same "awe, shucks" attitude that Japan had fallen in love with 66 years before, and the Iraqis had fallen in love with. A whole new generation of Japanese, in spite of the efforts to keep them hidden, to not provide them with office space, a placc to sleep, or food, fell in love with America's brightest and best who descended on northern Japan and helped to rebuild her in the days, weeks, and months following the disaster.

One of the most dramatic of the expeditions we sent out was to Jordan during the Gulf War of January-February 1991. The First Gulf War, as it is sometimes called, started shortly after midnight on January 15, 1991, when a US-led coalition began a campaign that had been authorized by the UN to expel from Kuwait Iraq forces that had invaded and occupied it in August 1990. The bombing, and the subsequent ground campaign of five days in February 1991, had created a steady stream of refugees from Iraq who poured into neighboring Jordan to escape the fighting. I decided that Agape House must take action. As frequently happened when we dispatched teams from Japan to disaster areas, we met with Japanese Foreign Ministry officials to discuss what we planned to do. After all, our teams were authentically Japanese and whatever they did would reflect Japan's image in the world.

"When are you planning to go?" a senior official asked me, his faced creased with fatigue from lack of sleep.

"Next Thursday," I said. The official grabbed the phone and barked a question into it. "When is the government plane departing?" he asked. He held the phone to his ear and waited for the reply. Then, still holding the phone and covering the mouthpiece with his hand he looked at me and asked, "How many of you plan to go to Jordan on this trip?"

"Thirteen," I said.

The official uncovered the mouthpiece and ordered, "Add an additional thirteen passengers." Then he put the phone down and smiled broadly. "There is a plane chartered by the Japanese government going to Amman next Thursday. "It is going to pick up refugees to take them back to the countries in Asia from which they originally came. It is a jumbo jet and it is practically empty. Since you are a team representing Japan, you can fly to Jordan for free."We made our preparations in the next few days and on the appointed Thursday were at Narita Airport, outside Tokyo, staring at a large and apparently almost empty Boeing Jumbo Jet. There were the 13 of us on the team, a bored Japanese Foreign Ministry official who was supervising the airlift, and 40 boxed lunches of Japanese food. The flight to Amman took twelve hours and we were driven from the airport straight to the refugee camp where we planned to work.

We had arranged with the refugee authorities on the ground in Amman to stay at a Jordanian government camp. For two months we worked at the camp, sorting out the relief supplies and distributing them to the refugees. But after several weeks of hard work our job was finished, and we all needed to return to Tokyo. The problem was, we hadn't a clue how to get back. The Japanese government-chartered Boeing 747 had long since completed its refugee evacuation flights and we were stranded.

But I wasn't in despair. As it happened, British recording company and airline entrepreneur Richard Branson had surfaced in the news recently because of his own charitable work with the refugees who had fled Iraq. In conversation with some of the team about what he had been doing, someone suggested that we contact him and see if he would come up with transportation for us. It was a long shot, but it was worth trying.

With the help of other members on the team in Jordan I managed to track down Branson's corporate phone number in London. An unnamed assistant listened to our story of having flown from Japan with a relief team and of needing a way to return the team to Japan. The assistant was polite but non-committal. Then he said he would transfer us to someone else. Several clicks later a cheery and easily recognizable voice with a strong British accent came on the line. "Hello," he said, "this is Richard. What can I do for you?"

At first I couldn't believe that it really was Richard Branson himself and I stammered around explaining who I was. Then I became more confident and gave him the background of our Japan-based relief teams. Finally I added, almost as an afterthought, "The challenge is that we have no way of getting our team back to Japan." I paused, took my heart in my mouth, and then asked, "Could you please help us get back to Japan?"

"That sounds great," he said jauntily. "I will work out the details with my secretary, Penny. Call back in a bit and we will arrange it." To my great surprise, when we did call back half an hour later, "Penny" answered the phone and said that everything had been arranged. All we needed to do was to get ourselves to London, which we did with Branson's help, staying in London for a couple days to rest and get the team together.

At Heathrow, the day after our arrival from Amman, we showed up at the Virgin Airlines ticket desk hoping that Penny had indeed forewarned them of our arrival. We needn't have worried, because to my great surprise Richard Branson himself was there to greet us and see us off. After working for several days in the hot and dirty refugee camps in Jordan, we certainly didn't look very good. Branson, however, escorted all thirteen of us into the first class section of the plane. Partly, I think, he was just being gracious. But partly also he wanted to assure the other first-class passengers on the plane, who had certainly paid several thousand pounds for the privilege of luxury air travel to Japan, that in spite of our scruffy appearance, he knew exactly who we were and he approved of us. For a few minutes, he stood at the front of the first-class section, speaking through a microphone to all the passengers on the plan and telling them that we had been performing "splendid" work in Jordanian refugee camps. "I want to congratulate them," he said, and the other first class passengers gave us a warm round of applause. Branson said a breezy "cheerio," and then was gone.

Two more major national catastrophes in Japan required the attention of the Emergency Team that had been formed when I returned to Japan from the US. One was a natural disaster: the Kobe earthquake of January 1995; and the second was the deadly sarin gas terrorist attack on the Tokyo subway system in May 1995 by Aum Shinrikyo, a sinister Japanese cult.

I learned of the earthquake at 5.45 in the morning when I was on the treadmill at the Clark Hatch athletic club in downtown Tokyo. Others in the gym stopped what they were doing when they caught sight of the TV screen nearest to them, assuming at first that it was a weather report. But after everyone watched for a few more seconds it quickly became apparent that the breaking news was a 7.3 earthquake in Kobe, 400 miles to the south of Tokyo.

The Agape House team in Japan had been re-organized into a Japan Emergency Team. Very soon after I had been mesmerized in the gymnasium by the footage coming from Kobe, I began to receive calls on my cell phone from other team members asking what they could do to help. I went home immediately, collected some personal things in a bag, and was soon on a train to Kobe with several other team members. We made it as far as Nagoya, responding en route to media phone calls and requests for interviews. In Nagoya we changed trains and arrived in Osaka around 5.00 p.m. Some team members who were already there met us at the station and began to drive us to Kobe. What would normally have been a ride of 20 minutes turned into a journey of nearly two hours.

On arrival, we were stunned by the absolute silence among the ruins. It had obviously been one of the worst earthquakes in Japan's recent history. People were huddled for warmth around fires burning on the streets in the January chill. There was a pall of gray dust over the city that seemed to be a sort of funeral shroud.

We drove first to the Emergency Center of Osaka Prefecture, but no one was there, so we then drove to City Hall, found a desk that no one was using, and set up our offices. We soon found that we had entered the world of the Internet, as our emergency numbers were being flashed on the screen by CNN and BBC stories of the quake. In response to the appearance of those numbers, we took more than 3,000 calls from people both in Japan and in other parts of the world who were desperate to locate family members in Kobe. We managed to patch through many of those calls to the relatives who were being sought. The team would make the call to the relative and do one of two things. If the family member could be located at one of the housing centers we would pass on the information to him or her. Otherwise, one of the team members would ride over on a bicycle to their address and leave them a note to call their family.

The sarin gas attack in May of the same year was terrifying. I had returned to Tokyo from the Kobe earthquake and was walking towards the metro station closest to my office which was in the centre of Tokyo and was called Kamiyacho. As I approached the station and prepared to enter it, it suddenly erupted with a cascade of Japanese stumbling and staggering out of it and then collapsing, one by one, on the sidewalk.

No one in the vicinity at first could figure out what had happened. We assumed immediately that there might have been a bomb explosion, yet no one had heard anything like that. The people who had collapsed outside the entrance, however, were throwing up. The only thing I could think to do was to turn them over on their stomachs so that they wouldn't choke on their own vomit. Within just a few seconds—and this led some people to believe that there was official foreknowledge of the attack—government security forces in plain clothes arrived. A group of us continued moving among the distraught, vomiting victims of the attack, checking to ensure that they were still alive. In the background the sirens of emergency vehicles of the fire department and medical agencies wailed away. We helped move some of the metro passengers to the ambulances if they seemed in any way ambulatory. The emergency medical personnel on the scene seemed overwhelmed by the incident. I heard someone in the background shouting "Sarin" and "Aum," the first word in the name of the bizarre and ultimately homicidal religious sect Aum Shinrikyo.

Aum Shinrikyo had been formed by a half-blind Japanese meditation specialist, Shoko Ashahara, who had organized a group that practiced an eclectic mixture of Buddhist and Daoist doctrines. It viewed the end of the world as imminent and its teachings emphasized the worship of Shiva, the Hindu god of destruction, and an apocalyptic catastrophe that would prepare the world for the reign of the Aum Shinrikyo cult. Disturbingly, Aum had not only acquired the approval of global figures like the Dalai Lama, but had managed to purchase quantities of firearms from Russia in the chaos of the post-Communist era. Of course, Aum was virulently anti-America and in the Japanese context, anti-establishment. It was believed by many that, in addition to many Japanese intellectuals who were drawn to its apocalyptic doctrines, some of the members were embittered members of the Burakumin criminal underclass in Japan. Several minutes after the initial chaos outside the Tokyo subway exit, some order seemed to emerge. Several of the bystanders and I, who had been drawn in to help after the exodus of coughing people from the subway, now realized that we had also been affected by the gas because we had been in close contact with victims of the attack. I underwent several medical check-ups in the next few days, and even now from time to time I succumb to various physical problems that all of the victims of the attack have been suffering since then. These include occasional instances of shortness of breath, interminable headaches, and indeterminate body aches. I am actually member number 517 of Tokyo's Subway Sarin Attack Victims Association. Many Japanese were injured in the terrorist attack. The government, after much wrangling in the media discussions of the issue, did open up its coffers to provide compensation for the attack. My first check came up to an amount around $510. That, however, would not have been enough to compensate the families of the twelve people who lost their lives in the nightmare of the attack. Many continue to this day to suffer from after-effects of various forms, most of them from nerve and breathing disorders.

CHAPTER FOUR

THE KIRISHITAN

O NE DAY IN the office, I came across a book called *A History of Christianity in Japan* by Henry Drummond. In spite of having grown up as a Christian in Japan, I knew little about the arrival, with Portuguese explorers, of the early Jesuits in the 16th century. The book indicated that by the year 1600 AD Christianity was the largest organized religion in Japan and the indiginous Japanese Christians were called the "Kirishitan." I had attended a Japanese school but had been taught nothing about the rich Renaissance-era history of Christianity in the country. I read voraciously about the rise of Christianity, then of its complete suppression in Japan. The final clampdown began in 1637 after the son of Hideyoshi Ieyasu, the recently established new military dictator of Japan, the Tokugawa Shogun, crushed a rebellion against his rule. Christians played a major role in that rebellion.

I knew vaguely that the Christian church went completely underground for an incredible two and a half centuries, only being "rediscovered" when American Protestant missionaries came to Japan after Commodore Matthew Perry and his "black ships" forced Japan in 1859 to open its doors to the outside world after two centuries of self-imposed isolation. A handful of "hidden" Japanese Christians, *Kirishitan* as they were called, approached early missionaries who came to Nagasaki not long afterwards and made it clear that Christianity, incredibly, had survived underground in Japan for two and a half centuries.

Since I returned to Japan to build up the Agape House work on Japanese soil I am often invited to different parts of the country to speak. I got into the habit of asking, after I had delivered my speech, if there were any Japanese Christian artifacts in the area. I was astounded to discover that in almost every part of the country I found evidence of "hidden Christians," graves, crosses, and other paraphernalia of underground Christianity. To my amazement I learned that Kyoto, the quintessentially Buddhist Japanese city, had in the year 1597 been the center of Christianity in Japan. According to Japanese historian Masaru Anesaki in his 1930 book, *The History of Japanese Religion*, more than 30 percent of the population of Japan at that time lived in Christian villages. As was dramatized in the 1931 movie "27 Martys," in 1596 there was a devastating earthquake in Kyoto to which the city's Christians, in sharp contrast to the Buddhist monks of the city, responded with generous offerings of rice and other food, and took it upon themselves to bury the dead and to take care of the wounded. The Japanese Kirishtan, according to accounts of the earthquake, provided assistance only to those who could pay for it. Not surprisingly, Christianity spread swiftly throughout the country as ordinary Japanese realized that the Christian God was "free."

Though the first Tokugawa Shogun of the new dynasty, Hideyoshi Iyeasu, favored the Christians and had not responded to Buddhist demands that they be suppressed, his son, Iemitsu, began a brutal persecution that resulted in the deaths of thousands of Japanese Christians by crucifixion, hanging or other forms of execution. This brutal and murderous suppression of the Japanese Christians was one of the longest and most savage national-level periods of persecution in Christian history. Only when missionaries began searching for the "hidden Christians" after the opening of Japan did they discover that, in spite of close surveillance of them and of the Japanese *Kirishitan,* some had survived the two and a half century bloodletting. But the Portuguese Jesuits who brought Catholicism to Japan in 1549 were not even the first missionaries to Japan.

I learned this by listening—so many times that it made me roll my eyes—as my dad related the story to all newcomers to Japan of how he crossed the Pacific by passenger ship in 1951 as an arriving missionary. Then a stripling of 22, he had bumped into the then owner of the *Japan Times*, Kikumatsu Togasaki. "Why are you going to Japan?" the distinguished-looking elderly publisher had asked my dad. Dad said that he was responding to the call by General MacArthur for 10,000 young people to come over to Japan and help the country as it slowly began to recover from the war. "That is wonderful," Mr. Togasaki had said, "and where in America are you from?"

"From Chicago," said my father.

But Togasaki wasn't finished with this enquiry. "But where are you *originally* from?" he asked.

"We are Assyrians," my dad replied, and explained that his father and mother had come to the US as refugees from the Assyrian Holocaust in Iraq that had begun in 1914.

Mr. Togasaki suddenly became animated. "Can I tell you something very important?" he said. "If you are an Assyrian it is not an accident that you are going to Japan. It was your people, the Assyrians, who brought to Japan the 'three treasures': Medicine, Freedom, and Christianity. Because of the foolishness of war, the three have been almost wiped out. We Japanese need you to walk in the footsteps of your ancestors and restore the three treasures to our country."

At the age of 22 and without any historical knowledge of the origins of Christianity in Japan, my dad quickly put the memory aside. It was not until years later, after having started a family, that he recalled what had happened and tried to contact Mr. Togasaki again. He learned that Togasaki had been dead several years. He decided to write a series of "letters to the editor" in various Japanese newspapers narrating this unusual story. If nobody responded to his letter, he thought, he would drop the matter.

He was astonished by the flood of responses he received. Not only did dozens of people confirm the story that Togasaki had told him, but he learned that the Assyrians had gone by the name of Keikyo. One of those who responded was Paul Saeki, author of several books about the Assyrians in China and other parts of Asia, and preeminent expert on Christianity in Asia. I myself didn't realize what an impact this discovery had made on my dad until I once phoned him from where I had been invited to speak in southern Japan. As was often the case, I wanted him to pray for the speaking engagement. I casually told him that there were many *Kirishitan* items in the neighborhood. "How dare you study those newcomers!" he said. Nonplussed at first, I asked him to explain. "You realize we are Assyrians?" he said. "We were here long before the *Kirishitan*. You should study the Assyrians." Since I was on the island of Kyushu, the southernmost of Japan's main islands, I decided to do some exploring on my own. My dad had often talked about the Assyrian sites in southern Japan. From as early as I could recall from his discussions about our Assyrian origins I remember his telling me that the Assyrian Christians had been responsible for Christianity's spread to vast expanses of the globe that had been entirely unfamiliar to Western Christendom. In fact, my dad had explained what amazing missionaries the Assyrian Christians had been, and how a sizeable portion of the world Christian community owed its salvation to them. I also recall fondly as a child visiting my Assyrian grandparents in Chicago, and being inundated with delicious dishes of "dolmas" and "kipti."

Now I was interested in pulling together the strands of this extraordinary story. The Assyrians had come from Assyria across the Silk Road and I wanted to learn how they had, in Mr. Togasaki's phrasing, brought "Christianity, freedom, and medicine."

I stopped in a small fishing village where the Assyrians had reportedly arrived. In the village, I found the shrine of Shintoism, the pre-Buddhist belief system of Japan. I had heard that it had originally been a church. By my dad's assertions, I thought it was crazy that the Assyrians had been there. Frankly, I wasn't convinced at all and was a little embarrassed. I decided to blurt out the assertion in the most direct way possible, hoping that the Shinto priest would be offended, would order me out of his shrine, and I would then be able to refute my dad's Assyrian claims thoroughly.

"My father tells me that this shrine was formerly a church. But that's ridiculous, isn't it?"

For a moment he was completely silent. Then he quietly said, "This is a strange shrine. Let me show you around it."

As we walked he said he himself didn't know the exact history of the Assyrians, but he had been assured that the harbor had been the arrival point for ships from the mainland of Asia during the first few centuries of the Christian era. The Japanese in this area, he explained, had referred to the Assyrians as the Hata people. I was dumbfounded that here, in this shrine of the Shinto faith, there were crosses carved into the rocks of the shrine. At the back of the shrine he showed me an ancient mask supposedly worn by the ancient Assyrians. It looked just like my dad.

When we finished, the Shinto priest said to me: "If you really want to find out more, you need to visit Kyoto." He pulled out one of his cards and said, "Let me write an introduction for you to visit the Koryuji Temple there." I found it very strange that a Shinto priest was writing me an introduction to a Buddhist temple. The next day, I went to Koryuji and met with the priest's wife. When I showed her the card, she was very happy and said that the priest was a family member. I had not realized the degree to which those that had come across the Silk Road had impacted Japan. She proceeded to take me around the temple, much as the Shinto priest had done the previous day. The most important artifact in the Koryuji temple is the Buddha called the "Miroku Bosatsu" whose hand is formed into the same sign that the Assyrians use. When I hesitantly brought up the story that my father had told me about this temple previously being a church, instead of being ordered off the Temple property, like I expected, she said, "You're probably right. When this temple was first build in the year 601 AD, Kyoto, as the last stop of the Silk Road, was like any Asian city. There were black people and white people and temples, shrines, churches and mosques. Everything that was on the Silk Road was in Kyoto and Nara. In fact, what many people consider to be "Japanese" was only a third of what was in those cities. The Miroku Bosatsu is often referred to as the Messiah Buddha because this temple has a long tradition of belief in the Buddha coming back to save the people," she explained. "In contrast to other temples, which are usually dark and foreboding, this temple is bright and hopeful. It is very likely that it originally was a church. I wouldn't be surprised at all, knowing the times."

I returned sheepishly back to Tokyo to meet my dad.

"So how was it?" he asked.

"It was exactly like you said, and then some," I answered. The result of that trip was the first book that my dad and I wrote together, along with a wonderful scholar of Japanese and Assyrian culture from UCLA named Jan Hollingsworth. The book was called *Japan: The Nation of the Cross* published by a major Japanese publisher, Tokuma Shoten. It became a best-seller across Japan. We followed this book with two more volumes, *Lost Identity: The Story of How Christianity First Arrived in and Grew in Japan* (Kobunsha), and, *Japan: Nation of the Bible* (Tokuma Shoten), which was a sequel to the first book.

The Assyrians, of course, had come to Japan via China. In fact, when I first applied for a visa to China at the Chinese embassy in Tokyo, I received a vivid indication of how much appreciation there was for the Assyrians. I had—perhaps too casually—assumed that I could stroll into the embassy and simply have a visa stamped in my passport. (Actually, a Chinese visa is a piece of paper that is glued onto one's passport pages.) To my shock, I was told a visa would require several days of waiting. As I had a flight leaving that evening, at the counter in the entrance hall of the consulate, I was told I needed to see the vice-consul himself.

"Why do you want to go to China?" he asked in a manner that obviously required some explanation. Instead of giving him a long-winded explanation, I slipped in front of him a magazine article written in English, its title "A Church from the 7th Century Found in China."

He wasn't a bit surprised by this, and simply looked at me with a sort of beatific smile. "This is where you want to go?" he asked.

"Yes," I said.

"When do you need the visa by?"

My flight was only hours away so I gave him a time that barely would permit me to make it to Narita airport with two hours left before the flight. He said, "Come back then and your visa will be ready." When I came back a few hours later, my visa was indeed ready and the vice-consul wanted to talk. He took me to another room and I had one of the strangest conversations I had ever had in my life. It wasn't until later that I realized that the room was being monitored. He asked me about our "people," the Christians in China, and how they were doing. I began to realize that he himself was a Christian and that explained his dramatic response. As I left, he told me, "Today I can only give you a one-time visa. But when you are in China, please bring me back a letter from some of your people there, and I can provide you with a multiple entry visa so you can go back and forth as much as you like."

In fact, when I next returned to China in March 2000, I took Harald Bredesen with me. We were accompanied by two Chinese officials and we visited the Da Qin monastery outside of Xian which had been known for many years as the tower of a 7th century Christian church.

On the way to the pagoda, we passed an impressively-sized church by the roadside. Curious about it, Harald asked the officials if we could visit it. We climbed out of the van and wandered in, and as we were admiring all the decorations and the high wooden ceiling, several Chinese began entering the church. We hadn't noticed them before.

What are they doing here?" I asked one of the Chinese officials.

"They want you to speak."

"What about?"

"Well, this is a church. You should probably talk about God."

For the next two hours, Harald and I alternated in our preaching, which was translated consecutively by the officials. The crowd applauded frequently during the messages, but as I sat down, exhausted after I had finished my turn speaking, there was a strange mumbling from the crowd.

"What's that all about?" I asked one of the interpreters.

"They are upset that you have stopped speaking." I looked at Harald in amazement. Then someone from the Chinese congregation approached my accompanying official and said that we could rest for a moment while the congregation sang some hymns. Then we were on our feet again, Harald and I playing tag team as preachers. At last the pastor of the church showed up, accompanied by the mayor of the village.

What was most amazing to us was the attitude of the Christians. With the long history of Christianity they were not intimidated by the Communist officials and seemed to have the attitude, "We have been Christians for 2,000 years—you have been Communist for 60—we will obey your laws but don't tell us how to pray." The humble mayor seemed to reflect that exact feeling. The Christians were a majority, and crime and other problems seemed to be, according to him, dramatically low.

Two years later Jan Hollingsworth and I received news of the discovery of a Christian site from 86 AD. The news was published in the *People's Daily* of all places, the daily organ of the Chinese Communist Party. I traveled to Nanking and met with Wang Weifan, a retired professor from Nanjing Theological Seminary, who kindly took me to the Carved Stone Museum where he had discovered stone carvings from the Han Dynasty. These were on the carvings of a large number of Middle Eastern themed carvings of stories from the Bible that included the creation story, Adam and Eve, the birth of Jesus and more. The date of 86 AD was confirmed as the date of the tomb from which they came, which brought confirmation of Christianity being in China to within 22 years of the original dates that we had put in our books 64AD in China and 70 AD in Japan.

In fact, there is plenty of additional evidence that Christians—and among them Christians of Assyrian ethnic background—were crossing Asia, probably using the Silk Road, well before the famous Christian mission to the Tang Dynasty court of Taizong in 635, which is commemorated in a Chinese and Syrica inscription on the famous Nestorian Tablet of 581 AD recording the visit. (The tablet itself is now preserved and exhibited in the Forest of Stelae Museum in Xian, China.) In fact, the alphabet used by the Turkic-speaking Uighur peoples of Chinese Central Asia, before the arrival of Islam, was called Uighur, and had been borrowed from Syriac, the liturgical language of the Church of the East.

The most striking evidence is the enormous extent of missions carried out by the Church of the East. Sometimes, and inaccurately, referred to as the "Nestorian Church," the Church of the East for several centuries was by far the largest branch of Christendom, bigger than the Orthodox Church which settled in Constantinople and the Catholic Church which became overwhelmingly identified with the Roman Empire of the West. In eighth century AD the Church of the East had archdiocese and bishoprics throughout the Arab world and Asia, including India. The church had sprung up among Christians whose mother tongue was Aramaic and who were probably descendants of the

Assyrians whose powerful empire had conquered the Northern Tribes of Israel in 622 BC. It was first and foremost a Semitic church, not only because Aramaic was the lingua-franca of Christians in that area of Mesopotamia, but because Syriac, a written version of Aramaic, became the official ecclesiastical language of the church. Indeed, the world's first Christian kingdom was Osrhoene, which the modern-day Assyrians of Iraq justifiably claim as their own people-group.

The moniker "Nestorian" was applied to the followers of Nestorius, the archbishop of Constantinople, who was condemned as a heretic at the Council of Ephesus in 431 AD after challenging the patriarchate of Constantinople over the use of the word Theotokos ("Mother of God") to designate Mary, the mother of Jesus. Nestorius also differed with the authorities of the Orthodox Church based in Byzantium over the dual nature of Christ as both human and divine. Nestorius went into exile in Egypt, but the Christians of northern Mesopotamia, whose ecclesiastical focal point was Seleucia-Ctephison (in modern-day Iraq on the Tigris River) had already accepted the political sovereignty and protection of the Sassanid dynasty of Persia, the area's dominant power. Rejecting the authority of Christian churches in both the Byzantine Empire and Rome in the West, the Church of the East (which at the present time calls itself the Assyrian Church of the East), regarded the term "Nestorian" as a calumny. Retroactively, the church rejected the judgments against Nestorius of the Council of Ephesus.

The Assyrian Christians had survived the Arab Muslim conquest of what is today Iraq in the middle of the 7th century AD. The modern persecution of Assyrians began in the 1890s with its peak between 1914 and 1923 where nearly one-third of the Assyrians were killed. The Simele massacre between August 7th

1933 and August 11th 1933 in which up to 3,000 Assyrians were slaughtered in 63 Assyrian villages in the Dohuk and Mosul areas was one of the most terrible. It was the exodus after this that my grandparents had arrived in Chicago in the 1920's.

But it wasn't until I was in Washington, DC, in November 2002 that I began to make contact with modern Assyrians deeply concerned about what was about to happen in Iraq. I was in the US capital to arrange meetings with officials from the State Department in order to find out more about the Assyrians. I had been introduced to some officials at Foggy Bottom (as the State Department is universally known to Washington insiders) by a friendly officer at the American embassy in Japan who had read my stories about the Assyrians and their impact on the world. I was on the phone with an old family friend, John Nimrod, an Assyrian who had also lived in Chicago. Until his death in 2009, John was one of the most important Assyrian leaders in the community outside of Iraq. A wonderful Christian and passionate Assyrian, he led the Assyrian Universal Alliance, an umbrella organization of world-wide Assyrian organizations started in 1968. John treated me like a son and we were to become dear friends."Where are you?" he asked.

"In Washington, DC," I said.

"Then get on a plane and come to London. We are having an important conference of Assyrians here and if you want to get to know our community, you need to be here." I sensed that this might be really important, so I booked a non-stop United flight to London.

When I arrived at Heathrow Airport I was met by members of a group called the Assyrian Universal Alliance. We stayed at a hotel adjoining Heathrow Airport and attended a large conference discussing the future of the Assyrian people that was being held there. I met many of my father's old friends and from many of them I learned more of the history of my ancient people, a people and a nation about which I had only really heard from my father up to this point. One of the attendees at the conference was Yonadam Kanna, who was later to become a member of the Governing Council, the embryonic core of what became the post-liberation government of Iraq. A well-built, graying man in late middle age, Kanna demonstrated a decisive manner and showed himself familiar both with what was happening in Iraq and what the likely outcome of the US-led invasion would be.

At the conference there were Assyrians who had been briefed by officers in the US military, and they told us how we might expect the imminent conflict in Iraq to affect the Assyrians. In parallel with the Assyrian conference was another conference of Iraqi opposition groups being held in a hotel near-by. Many of them went on to become leaders of the post-Saddam government. John Nimrod often slipped away to attend these meetings, where, unbeknown to us, the basics of what would happen to the Assyrians during the invasion and post-Saddam agenda in Iraq were being stitched together.

As the conference drew to a conclusion, John Nimrod asked me if I would come back to Washington with him and attend some meetings. The two of us, along with another Assyrian who doesn't want himself identified, met with a number of State Department officials who were in charge of planning the by-now almost certain US invasion of Iraq. The briefing was detailed and we were given considerable information on how the war might affect the Assyrians. I asked the official briefing us a simple question. "What happens after the war is over?"

He responded that post-war planning was still under consideration. This was a very unsettling reply.

We ourselves knew little of the actual situation, let alone the military planning, but when we would repeatedly ask about the post-war situation in Iraq, it struck us as really strange that officials at the State Department, at least, gave no indication that there had been extensive serious planning at all. It seemed to John Nimrod and the rest of us that the post-war situation would be the most important part of the operation.

I wanted to know how, in particular, Iraq's significant Assyrian community—about 2.5 million out of approximately 25 million or roughly 10 percent of the population—would function. While there had been massive and thorough preparations for the military part of the invasion, there had been disturbingly little attention given to what the post-war situation might be like. Much of what planning was done, in fact, seemed to have been done in the rough. I felt then, and still feel, that this was a huge and critical mistake. It was to have disastrous repercussions in the months and years to come. Walking out of the C Street main entrance to the Department of State building in Washington, DC, we mulled the first hint that something was very wrong.

CHAPTER FIVE

IRAQ AFTER THE INVASION

THE DRIVE TO Amman after we exited Iraq just days before the invasion was fatiguing and brutal. I wanted to get into action immediately to arrange for aid to be brought back into Iraq once the war had begun and then come to an end. One of the first people I went to meet in Amman was Hajem Hallaseh, director of the Near East Foundation, one of the Middle East's oldest NGOs (non government organization) which had been established early in the 20th century. Hallaseh was a pleasant man in his forties who had worked with our group of Japanese volunteers during the Gulf War in 1991. He couldn't imagine why the Iraqis, who had always been the rich cousins to the Jordanians, would need Jordan's help now that the war was on us. But he knew I was serious about going back into Iraq to help the Iraqis after the Americans and the British had liberated them from Saddam.

Once the war began less than three days after my arrival in

Amman, there was soon news that Saddam had fled the Iraqi capital. By April 9 the Americans had moved in and conquered Baghdad. I sent out word to our Japanese volunteers to make their way to Amman to prepare to take relief supplies into Iraq. We also needed to stir up support within Jordan for our relief efforts. When the Japanese kids arrived, as we had done many times in the past, we visited various Jordanian newspapers and TV and radio stations to ask for help with supplies to take to Iraq once the war was over. We had no funds and no supplies. We asked them to put out an appeal for food, medicine, trucks, blankets, and for anyone wanting to send a letter to their family members in Iraq.

Our plea for help through the media generated an immediate effect. Our Jordanian mobile phone received constant calls from Jordanians volunteering to help. A Jordanian trucking company offered to lend us as many trucks as we needed to take supplies into Iraq. The manager of the trucking company, Al Jazy, had lived in the United States and had fond recollections of his time there. I think also that the warm Jordanian response was because ordinary Jordanians were humbled that so many volunteers were flying in from far-away Japan to help neighboring Iraqis whom, after all, the Jordanians ought themselves to be helping.

We also needed to secure accommodations for the volunteers, and I found myself wandering from hotel to hotel making my pitch. Finally, one of the two Japanese students who had been in Iraq before the war began located a Palestinian-owned hotel improbably called "The Toledo." Here again, the Palestinian owner had warm memories of growing up in the US and offered to let us have rooms in the hotel for a huge room discount and to use the hotel address for Iraqis to send their letters from inside or outside the country.

Now I faced a different problem. I learned that the American bombing had destroyed the Iraqi telephone exchange and that it was almost impossible for Iraqis in their own country to communicate with each other. Once the volunteers and I were back in Baghdad we would need reliable telephones to keep in contact with each other, as well as the outside world. Someone had seen billboards around Amman advertising a new satellite phone company called Thuraya. We contacted the president of the company by email in Dubai where his headquarters were and asked for ten satellite phones to take to Baghdad.

To my surprise and delight, I received an immediate response and the promise of delivery of ten satellite phones and as much calling time on them as we might need. The phones, and the availability of the Toledo Hotel as a mailbox for Iraqis trying to keep in contact with each other, turned out to be a vital transitional stage between the total destruction of war and the beginning of the restoration of basic services. Our Japanese student volunteers, meanwhile, were gathering up all the material supplies we would take back into Iraq. At the same time, I was eager to contact a friend whom I knew was staying at the Amman Intercontinental Hotel to let him know what the situation in Iraq had been like just before the war began. I felt it was important to correct the impression held by many people in the world that the war was unjust and that the Americans had invaded the country merely to get hold of the oil or perhaps, more absurdly, to compensate for the fact that President George H.W. Bush, who had engineered the impressive international coalition against Iraq during the first Gulf War, had failed to make it all the way to Baghdad.

I called the Intercontinental and was transferred by the operator to what I presumed to be my friend's room. Barely allowing the person at the other end of the line to say hello, I began to pour out my story of the desperate situation that Iraqis had been in just prior to the war. When I paused after a few moments to catch my breath, the voice on the other end of the line said, "Excuse me, whom are you trying to reach?"

When I mentioned the name of my friend he answered, "I'm sorry, but I think you may have the wrong room number. My name is Arnaud de Borchgrave. I am the editor of UPI and I would love to hear your story."

Nobody needed to explain to me who Borchgrave was. A Belgium-born former *Newsweek* correspondent, he had interviewed everyone including President Nasser and the Israeli Prime Minister Levi Eshkol (in the same year), and then, most famously, in 1972, at the height of the Vietnam War, North Vietnam's Politburo member and Premier Pham Van Dong. In 1985 he had become editor-in-chief of the *Washington Times*. When I found myself inadvertently speaking to him in March 2003, he was editor-at-large of the *Washington Times* and the famous American wire service UPI (United Press International).

For anyone interested in reporting and in global trouble spots, Borchgrave was a household name. In fact, I had briefly met him in Tokyo years before. We now met in the lobby of Amman's Intercontinental Hotel a few minutes after our phone conversation. I assumed that I would be spending a few minutes over tea with him. In fact, the conversation I had with him turned into a story that reverberated around the world through UPI and eventually ended up on the White House website as an article under my own byline with the title, "I Was Wrong!"

What was most significant about it was that it was the first account of someone who had been in Baghdad immediately before the war and made clear that many Iraqis were literally longing for the war to begin because they disliked Saddam Hussein so much. Amid a generally cynical view of the American invasion of Iraq by many Western reporters, here I was telling the world that I had met dozens of Iraqis who had desperately wanted the Americans to attack. It was certainly counter-intuitive. Within hours of the appearance of my story "I Was Wrong!" on the UPI wires, I began to receive phone calls from all over the world by people who had contacted Arnaud. Suddenly, here was someone with direct reporting experience confirming what the US administration had been saying was true: the Iraqis really wanted liberation by the Americans from Saddam Hussein. One person who contacted me through Arnaud was a Hollywood agent wanting to do a movie. But more importantly than this, I was inundated with requests for interviews from every conceivable news organization.

One Internet website tried to discredit my reporting by arguing that I had not been known as an anti-war protester, that there were no examples of my expressing anti-war views before the war began. It also tried to smear Borchgrave and the *Washington Times*, digging up long-stale complaints about the newspaper's founder, Rev. Moon, the South Korean founder of the Unification Church, which many people regard as a quasi-Christian cult. In fact, I had expressed anti-war views very vigorously in Japanese before I visited Iraq, something that the skeptics of my anti-war views could not have known. But at least one former human shield participant, Daniel Pepper, had written an article for Britain's *Daily Telegraph* newspaper entitled "I Was a Naïve Fool to be a Human Shield for Saddam." Pepper, a writer and photo journalist originally from Cleveland,

Ohio, described in his piece an Iraqi taxi-driver looking at him with an expression of incredulity when the peace activist repeated his mantra, "Bush bad, war bad, Iraq good." Pepper says that at this point the driver slowed his cab down and, in broken English, spoke of the evils of the Saddam regime. "Now this guy was telling me," Pepper had said in the *Daily Telegraph* article, "how all Iraq's oil money went into Saddam's pocket and that if you opposed him politically he would kill all your family." Along with five other Western human shields, Pepper had hired a cab to take them to Amman. On the way, Pepper said, the driver (different from the first one to whom Pepper had spoken), began to unload. Pepper wrote, "We just sat, listening, our mouths open wide. Jake, one of the other [human shields], just kept saying, 'Oh my God,' as the driver described the horrors of the regime. Jake was so shocked at how naïve he had been. We all were. It hadn't occurred to anyone that the Iraqis might actually be pro-war."

I learned from this experience the hard way that news has its own priorities. One of the interviewers desperately trying to reach me was ABC's Barbara Walters. She wanted to do a one-hour piece, but the condition was that it would have to be exclusive. Reluctantly, I turned down offers for interviews from CNN, the BBC, CBS, ITN in the UK, and NBC News. I was asked to bring over to the ABC studios rented for the occasion by the network all the videos I had smuggled out of Iraq. Sadly, I never saw them again.

But it was not to be. A late-breaking story pushed my interview off for that night. As for BBC, NBC, ITN and the rest, they had already long since moved on to other things. The fact is, however, I seemed to be one of the very few people telling the story of how wretched most Iraqis had felt under Saddam.

A couple of days after the fiasco with Barbara Walters, Arnaud called and said that he was being interviewed by Fox News and wanted me with him. I not only told the story of plight of the Assyrian Christians but held up an Assyrian flag that, with great terror, one of my Assyrian friends had given to me clandestinely when I had been in Baghdad. For this crime alone, under Saddam, he could have received the death penalty. As I held the flag up in front of the Fox News TV cameras, Assyrians around the world saw the Assyrian flag displayed in public for the first time. I am still known in some quarters as "the guy who first showed the world the Assyrian flag." That display of the Assyrian flag brought encouragement and hope to Assyrians worldwide.

I had suddenly become a news source who was much in demand around the world. But in addition to fielding interview requests, I was working myself into the ground, along with my Japanese volunteer team, preparing the supplies we wanted to take into Iraq. In the midst of all this I received a call from CNN. The producer said that CNN had been interviewing Iraqis in Amman who said the only people trying to help them were "the Japanese." When the correspondent showed up for the interview, I was delighted to see that the lady was Rym Brahimi, someone I'd met several times during my time in Baghdad and told how much the Iraqis wanted to be rid of Saddam Hussein. Rym had herself been expelled from Iraq before hostilities started and knew only too well what life had been like. She and her crew took footage of our offices of the Japan Emergency Team, of the signs being prepared to be mounted on the side of the truck we would take in, and all of the letters that had made it to the Toledo hotel, as well as the messages that had been taken by phone for Iraqis inside Iraq.

Rym and her crew followed us to the truck where we were loading supplies. On the way to Baghdad, stopping at one of the rest stops in Jordan, we watched her program be broadcast on CNN. Before we got that far, however, we had a big problem to solve. The situation on the Iraqi side of the border was still very unstable, and moving vehicles along the road ran the risk of being bombed by the Americans. The day before, a bus load of people en route to Baghdad had been bombed. Yet the Japanese kids were chafing at the bit to get into the country. They were anxious to deliver the more than 500 letters from family members that had arrived at the Toledo hotel as well as deliver supplies of medicine, clothing, and food. They also wanted to set up the satellite phones we had been supplied. It was apparent from sketchy news reports that Iraq's entire communication structure had broken down even as hostilities were drawing to an end. I tried to contact the American embassy to let the diplomats there know that our convoy would be one of the first to cross the border with relief supplies once the fighting stopped. We didn't want to be bombed by accident.

What complicated the process was that we had to make our contacts through the State Department in Washington, DC. But the State Department officials wouldn't be open with us about how safe the road into Baghdad would be. We were not receiving any confirmation that it would be safe to depart from Amman. I had a late-night discussion with the Japanese kids and they made the point that for every hour we delayed people might be getting sick or even dying in Iraq. When I awoke the following morning there was a note next to my bed that read, "Sorry we couldn't wait anymore. We decided to go ahead."

I took a taxi in a great rush to where the truck had been loaded and discovered it had already gone. Apparently the Japanese had convinced the driver, who was waiting on standby for orders that it was okay to leave right away with or without me. I had a nightmarish vision of a two-ton truck filled with Japanese young people bombed to pieces on the road to Baghdad, so I immediately found a taxi that was willing to make the Baghdad run and sped along after them. Since the car was considerably faster than the truck, I felt that I had a good chance of catching them. At the border the Jordanian guards thought they had recently witnessed the funniest scene imaginable, a large truck with eight Asian youths asleep in the open atop the supplies. They told me that they had checked everyone's papers, found no discrepancies and had let the Japanese through.

"Oh, they were your kids! We should have known," they laughed again as I protested the evident irresponsibility of the immigration officials at the border. "We should have known," they said, "because we knew them well from past crossings." As the car in which I was being driven made its way onto the Iraqi side of the border, I realized that a huge change had taken place. Though the gigantic pictures of Saddam Hussein were in place, as they had been on the previous trip, the offices at the border were completely empty and seemed to have been stripped of everything of any value. There was nobody at the border and in contrast to the last time we had crossed where there had been extreme checking, it was a ghost town.

As the driver forged ahead towards Baghdad I kept a sharp lookout of the car windows on the search for anything resembling an American tactical aircraft that might have been patrolling the road. I was also desperate to catch sight of the truck, which by now must be several miles ahead of the taxi.

There were plenty of bombed out vehicles as I approached the borders of Iraq, and even the remains of a bus that had been bombed. But there was no sign of any truck. I kept praying for protection for the kids as I got farther into Iraq. Then, about half-way between the Jordanian border and Baghdad, just before we got to Fallujah, I saw the truck in the distance. There it was, loaded to the gills with supplies, with Japanese young people who formed part of the Japan Emergency Team fast asleep atop the supplies. We overtook the truck and motioned to the driver to pull over. He looked more scared than I was. As the truck slowed to a halt the eight youths all awoke with a start. *"Gomen!"* ("Sorry!"), they shouted over the sound of the truck's engine. "We couldn't wait any longer. We kept thinking of all those Iraqis in desperate need and even dying."

I was furious at the decision they had made without any consultation with me—who after all, had initiated the entire operation. But I couldn't help feeling immensely proud of their courage and commitment. I bellowed at them that they could all have been killed, but my cheeks were running with tears. These kids cared so much that they hadn't given a thought to their own safety. But they had an interesting tale to tell. As they had crossed the border in the middle of the night, two unidentified helicopters had lit up the truck with a searchlight and flew overhead until it was daylight. It was as if the helicopters were protecting them. We never did find out what American unit they were from or how they had known about the truck carrying relief supplies, but to us it was a miracle. I crammed as many of the kids as I could into my car while the rest remained on the truck the remainder of the way to Baghdad.

Bombed-out vehicles littered the entire roadside. There had been plenty of stories about the wholesale American destruction of much of the city, but everything—at least as far as I could tell from the buildings—looked surprisingly normal. But things weren't normal for the Iraqis. As we drove into town that April 17, just nine days after an American military vehicle had dragged off a pedestal the statue of Saddam in the middle of Baghdad, a week after the liberation, Iraqis from adults to children, the young, the elderly, came rushing out asking for water. The truck slowed down to a walking pace for several blocks as the Japanese kids threw out bottles of water to the people who had also showed up at the sight of relief supplies. We had taken a chance on making the decision that the vast bulk of the supplies we brought in consisted of drinking water, and we had been right.

Our Japan Emergency Team had been the first relief truck to cross the border after the fighting stopped, and there was an increasingly festive atmosphere as we drew closer into the city. Exuberance on the faces of everyone was palpable. It seemed as if much of the population of Baghdad was on the streets enjoying the toppling of their long-time dictator. We were worried, though, because so many people were trying to surround the truck and get supplies. We sensed possible danger if the pandemonium got out of hand.

Driving up to the Palestine Hotel and the Sheraton Hotel, we couldn't help noticing the sense of sheer joy among people on the streets. In front of the Palestine Hotel there were throngs of people who just seemed exultant that they could say what they wanted to say about the just-ousted Saddam Hussein regime. Here were Iraqis, free at last after forty years of brutal political oppression, and they certainly wanted to be seen celebrating. There were people literally dancing in the streets.

The Palestine hotel had become the temporary headquarters of the US forces in the city. People swarmed around it in the highest spirits. Many of them were asking for help from everyone and anyone who would listen. Every conceivable civic, social, or political group which had been suppressed or destroyed under the Saddam regime was there, many with signs and posters that they had not been able to show in public for decades.

We drove around Baghdad trying to find the headquarters of the Assyrian Church of the East. When we found it close to the center of downtown Baghdad, the office staff of the church rushed out to hug me and the Japanese kids. Then a second-floor window of the building swung open and the Archbishop of Iraq, Mar Gewargis, shouted at me with a big smile, "Why didn't you call?" He recognized me from a few weeks earlier.

"I did, but you wouldn't answer the phone!" I joked. We both knew that the phone service in Baghdad had been down for more than a month.

All of us, having finally made it safely into downtown Baghdad, were exhausted, especially after the long and uncomfortable trip across the desert from Amman. The staff of the Church of the East graciously provided refreshments for us as everyone in the truck and the car gratefully got out and stretched their limbs.

Our biggest hit on the truck—at least as far as Mar Gewargis was concerned—was the satellite phones. We distributed one of them to the archbishop and made preparations to move the Japanese kids into accommodations provided by Father Yeshua at the Mar Gwargis Church, the closest to the headquarters. The whole Assyrian community, along with their trusted friends and neighbors, then helped us distribute the twenty tons of water, medicine, food, blankets, and additional satellite phones. That took most of the day, and we finished just in time for the driver and the borrowed truck to make the return trip to Amman.

With the unloading completed, I took time to observe what was happening in Baghdad. The ever-present portraits of Saddam, the statues and the billboards glorifying the Iraqi leader, had all been defaced or pulled down. There was a sense of excitement in Iraq similar to that of a community whose home team has just won the league championship. Some Iraqis continued for several days to dance with joy in the streets. It was difficult to believe that Baghdad's problems were only just beginning.

We met with Assyrian church leaders and organized a plan to distribute the relief supplies and set up the satellite phones and distribute the letters. We decided to distribute the seven remaining satellite phones among the several churches in Baghdad, but that each person would be limited to three minutes. Yet as soon as the announcement had gone out that such a service would be available, huge lines began to form around the churches as people waited to make their first call to their relatives. Meanwhile, the food, clothing, medicine and water we had supplied were kept closely watched at Father Yeshua's St. Gewargis Church. St. Gewargis is Arabic for St. George, the patron saint of the Assyrians. It seemed as though everybody from the Archbishop to the lowliest layperson in the church and just about everyone in between was called "George."

We still had the task of delivering the letters. Even though Father Yeshua proposed that the letters be assigned among the seven churches that also possessed the satellite phones, the Japanese kids were insistent on delivering the letters personally. In typical Japanese fashion they felt responsible for delivering the letters themselves and picking up a return letter.

It was a huge job because there were more than 500 letters, but the Japanese focused on this as their main task, helped by people from the seven churches. In addition to delivering the letters, the kids hung around long enough to take back to Amman replies to those letters. The mail delivery process took nearly a month.

Meanwhile, the satellite phones were becoming a major attraction of Baghdad. There were several hundred people lined up each morning outside the churches, eager to let their

relatives know that they were okay. It was a challenge to confine the conversations to three minutes, but the Japanese young people were certainly intent on trying, along with the wonderful Assyrians who were so excited now what Saddam was gone and that the brave Americans were there for them.

One of the first Assyrian Christians to emerge as a leader in all of this was Fred George A young man in his thirties who had served in the Iraqi army, he was one of the leaders at the Assyrian church and was also involved with the Assyrian Democratic Movement. He was strong and muscular, and had an inescapable leadership presence. He quickly took charge of all of the provisions kept at Father Yeshua's church and dramatically improved the distribution system. He suggested to me that I might like to meet the workers of the newly opened Assyrian Center at the center of Baghdad.

It turned out that the building under Saddam had been a torture center of one of the numerous Iraqi security agencies, but it had now been turned over to the Assyrian Democratic Movement. As was the case in much of Baghdad in the days immediately following the downfall of the regime, it was a scene of emotional meetings, hugs and celebrations. I quickly re-established my acquaintance with Yonaddam Kanna, whom I had met in London a few months earlier. He was as happy as all the others, but he said something that stopped me dead in my tracks and that would come back and haunt me many times later. "Amir," he said, "of course we are happy and we are grateful to the Americans for liberating us. But we know the Americans. They are impatient. They will be with us for a few years, but then they will leave and we will be worse off than before."

I was hurt and angry when I heard this. In fact, I felt like rounding on him for his ingratitude at having been liberated by the Americans. I protested, using his nickname, "Yako, how can you say such a thing?" I fired back at him. "The Americans have forced Saddam Hussein out of power. Iraq is finally free again. How ungrateful of you to say something as dismissive of the Americans as that."

He gave me an odd smile and said, "I know. Just you watch."

I did. And events seemed to prove him right.

CHAPTER SIX

OMINOUS CHANGES

OUR JAPANESE VOLUNTEERS continued to work with energy and diligence in distributing both the supplies and the letters. There were twenty tons of supplies and about five hundred letters. People couldn't get enough of the satellite phones, of course, and the lines around the seven churches persisted. A friend of mine, Fred, had heard, meanwhile, that the American occupation headquarters were no longer at the Palestine Hotel where they had first set themselves up, but in one of Saddam's downtown Baghdad palaces. Some ten days after the team had arrived in Iraq with supplies, I decided to see what was going on and he and I drove over in his car. Without so much as a glance from anybody connected with security, we drove into the courtyard of the building and parked outside what appeared to be the headquarters. Asking around a little, we both learned that a daily briefing would be held shortly in Saddam's main Baghdad residential palace which had been turned into the headquarters of the US Operations. I wanted among other things to learn what was going to be done to satisfy the needs of the Assyrian Christians. We learned that the meeting would take place each day at 5.00 p.m. and we made it a habit, whenever possible for the next few months, to attend it. Two days later, we showed up and were ushered into a room with about ten representatives of various NGO's working now in Baghdad. There were several American military officers in attendance. One of the faces I noticed early on was that of Marla Ruzick, a brave American volunteer who was a fearless and passionate campaigner for the victims of violence. Three years earlier, she had founded Ruzicka, an organization called Campaign for Innocent Victims in Conflict. Marla had worked tirelessly to provide help for families caught up in the cross-fire of American military action in both Iraq and Afghanistan. A year almost to the day after we drove back into Iraq with a supply-loaded truck, she was killed when a roadside bomb hit the convoy in which she was traveling to the airport. When she died, she had been trying to arrange for the evacuation of an Iraqi teenager who was to be taken to the Bay area for surgery. Marla was truly one of the American angels whom we were falling in love with every day. As I took my place at the conference table in the middle of the briefing room, I saw two familiar faces on the other side of the table. They were two of the original human shields who had been present at that fateful church meeting when I had first learned how much the Assyrians hated the Saddam regime. They had been outspokenly hostile to the Americans from the first moment they had opened their mouths in the pre-invasion period. I was really rather angry at this blatant display of hypocrisy. I walked over and demanded to know why they were there. Sheepishly, they said that they "wanted to help." I figured that they had seen which way the wind was blowing with the Americans in charge and were hoping to receive assistance from the very Americans they had expressed themselves as hating so much. I then walked up to the head of the table and explained to the senior briefer who they were. They were quickly escorted from the room. I had seen how hypocritical some of the human shields had been, and I wanted no connection with such hypocrisy again.

The daily briefing was being held at what was called ORHA, the Office of Reconstruction and Humanitarian Assistance. Essentially, the Americans wanted to hear from various humanitarian groups, and to explain as well what they were doing in various areas of Iraqi national life. Teams would report, one by one, what they had been doing in the post-invasion Iraq to restore electricity, meet with emerging political figures, supervise food and medicine distribution, and so on. After the American officers presented their reports, we would report what we were doing. The senior official at this stage of the American presence was Lieutenant General Jay Garner who was later replaced by Ambassador J. Paul Bremer. ORHA remained in place until after Bremer's arrival on the 13th of May and became the Coalition Provisional Authority (CPA) at the end of May. General Garner departed the second week in June, two months beyond what had been the agreement with Donald Rumsfeld and President Bush. My impression, despite what later became the conventional judgment of Garner's supervision of the reconstruction efforts, was that the American officers were working hard and effectively to restore order in the capital. We were given daily reports on improvement in the electricity situation, the repair and building of hospitals, schools, and other needed agencies.Many of the Assyrians, with whom I closely identified, would arrive at the briefings with requests for assistance. They were trying to find out what had happened to missing relatives, which people's homes had been confiscated, and where they could get needed medical treatment.

Two concerns of many Iraqis came to the surface early on. Many wanted to know why the Iranians had been permitted to broadcast into Iraq in Baghdad almost from the beginning of the liberation period. I had noticed this as soon as I returned to Iraq in the second half of April from Jordan. At the end of each day's work we would come back and watch it, almost falling out of our chairs laughing at the reporting. "Please ask them to stop the TV from Iran," my Assyrian friends and relatives begged me. "It is nonstop and it is just driving us crazy." Every day for hours at a time there were endless reports of the Americans having raped hundreds of Iraqi women or killing thousands of ordinary Iraqis. It was so absurd that you couldn't help but laugh at the sheer immensity of the lies that were being told. Many Iraqis at the briefings in Saddam's palace were troubled by this hostile and plainly ridiculous propaganda against the Americans. Some wanted to know why the station couldn't immediately be blocked. They understood the cynical dictum of Joseph Goebbels, Hitler's propaganda chief, that if a lie were repeated often enough it would be believed.

We decided to take up the question of the Iranian TV reports being broadcast into Iraq from neighboring Iran. With Saddam's two TV stations off the air, amazingly neighboring Iran, the enemy of all that was happening in Iraq, had set up a 24-hour Arab broadcasting channel. With its slanderous and dishonest reporting, it was undermining the good that the Americans were doing. After weeks of asking around, I finally found someone who was ready to answer my questions. "Can't you jam these broadcasts?" I asked an official at one of the briefings. "They are doing untold harm."

"Due to international treaties," the official told me, "we are unable to jam broadcasts." I was dumbfounded. Here was the US government, having just entered someone else's country, toppled the regime, and begun to set up a government, pathetically asserting that "international treaties" prevented its blocking a television broadcast dedicated to undermining its presence in Iraq. Yet for a long time, the Iranian broadcasts, with their relentless spouting of hatred for the Americans, were the only TV signals the Iraqis could receive.

Despite the laughable nature of the broadcasts, clearly, a la Joseph Goebbels, the TV station was eroding the ability of the Americans to sustain support for their running the country; because the Americans never set up a television station of their own to communicate all the progress that was being made in Iraq. To this day, I believe that one of the greatest reasons for much of the difficulties in Iraq was a total failure to communicate in real time what the Americans were doing to rebuild Iraq, as had been done successfully a generation earlier in Japan. The justification Americans kept giving in response was that they did not want to encourage propaganda and wanted to nurture a free press in Iraq. While everybody agreed, in the face of a non-stop Iranian propaganda, there was an absolute need to communicate with the Iraqi people what was happening on a daily basis. Sadly, it was never done and the Iranian propaganda, over time, took its toll. I can't help thinking that this decision by the US was one of the stupidest of many miscalculated decisions in Iraq.

There were other indications of malice and social subversion from Iran. Within weeks of the liberation notices began to be posted on doors, in public places and everywhere in between. They read: "To the women of this House. Immediately cover your heads according to Islamic custom or you will have four choices. We will either bomb you, rape you, kill you or burn your House." All the Iraqis knew where the threats came from. The quality of the Arabic language used in the threatening notices indicated that it had been written by Iranians. A few weeks later, in early June 2003 Fred and I had the opportunity of taking a car and driving south out of Baghdad. Once we left Baghdad on our way to Samawah we began to realize that in place of the Iraqi flag we were seeing the green Shia flag. The farther South we traveled the more clearly we could see that in fact southern Iraqi in some ways had become "western Iran." Sometime after this we were to hear from many Iraqis that the Shiite cities of Karbala and Najaf, respectively 60 miles southwest and 100 miles south of Baghdad, were so full of Iranians that only Iranian money was being used. Local hotels had started refusing payment in Iraqi dinars and demanding payment in Iranian rials. It is important to note here that Karbala and Najaf are holy cities for Shia Islam, which is dominant in Iran and Iraq, and the ultimate goal for a Shia Islam is to be buried in one of these cities. Therefore, the Iraqis there were doing what could only be termed as a business, selling burial plots at inflated prices to Iranian pilgrims who were visiting the site. In many ways, the southern part of Iraq was becoming more and more a defacto part of Iran. The subject of the Iranians led naturally to the question of the country's borders. Several Iraqis and Assyrians told us that they were upset that the Americans had failed to take control of Iraq's borders and that there were many dangerous insurgents crossing into Iraq from Saudi Arabia, Iran, Jordan and Syria.

When we first raised the issue at the ORHA briefings—it had, after all, been brought to my attention by Iraqis themselves—any possible problem was completely denied. But we persisted in asking why the borders of Iraq were so porous and it was then I was rather brusquely told that I should stop asking the question.

"Why not?" I countered. "My fellow-Assyrians are deeply worried that, with no effective monitoring of the borders, those working to destabilize Iraq and deprive Iraqis of their newfound freedom will be free to come and go as they wish."

I persisted with my inconvenient questioning until we were finally taken aside by an American officer after one of the briefings who had come to the Assyrian compound to follow up with me.

"I cannot tell you anything," he began. "At the same time, I know you are sincere and need to convey to the Iraqis what the real situation is. Though I cannot say anything positively, you can ask me questions, and in reply I may ask you questions."

I was bewildered. What was he trying to hide? The officer kept insisting that the entire topic was classified and that he was not able to talk about it. Finally, I badgered him into an exasperated response as I kept coming back to the subject.

"Okay," he said, "I can't tell you anything positively, but you can ask me some questions and I can ask you some questions in reply. Okay?"

"All right," I said grudgingly. "Why don't you close the borders? Without control of the borders the very worst people in the world, precisely those who want to destroy the new-found freedom of the Iraqi people, are free to enter the country."

"Is it such a bad thing," the officer responded, "that all the bad people in the world want to come to Iraq?" He made a rather silly attempt to feign mock anger.

"Of course," I replied. "It's a disaster. Can't you see that?"

"Are you sure it's a disaster? Is it really such a bad thing?"

I thought this was becoming downright foolish. I couldn't imagine why he thought—or had been told to say—that it was fine and dandy that all the "bad people" were making their way into Iraq. Then I had a bizarre thought.

"You aren't saying that you are purposely letting the borders stay open so that all the bad people of the world can come into Iraq and then you can catch them?"

He suddenly looked rather cheerful. Instead of saying anything that might constitute the transmission of information to me, he smiled broadly and made a sign across his face as though he were zipping his lips up. This was amazing. If what he was suggesting were true, it would seem that Iraq's borders were being deliberately left unmonitored so that "the bad guys" would be attracted into Iraq like flies to honey. Wanting to kill Americans, they would be drawn into Iraq so that the Americans could catch them there. On the face of it, this seemed an absurd strategy and indeed it was to have terrible consequences for years to come. I believe it was another of the most critical blunders of the postwar administration of Iraq.

Well, if it was the policy of the US-occupying administration of Iraq to allow in—indeed to attract in—all the "bad people" of the surrounding countries, it was certainly working. Abu Musab al Zarqawi, the viciously cruel head of Al Qaeda in Iraq, who was to murder dozens of Iraqis and foreigners before finally being killed in an American airstrike, had happily made his way into the country from Jordan. The only trouble was, it was to take years before this "bad person" was caught. It wasn't until June 7, 2006, that Zarqawi was killed in an F-16 airstrike on a safe house where he was meeting with fellow-conspirators some 35 miles north of Baghdad. Several others, perhaps the majority of the militant Islamists who had entered the country, were never caught at all.

In many ways by June of 2003 things were improving on the ground. Early in July of 2003 there were rumors that Baghdad would soon be seeing direct flights to cities like London, Paris, and New York. We were all excited an]d I was touched that the Iraqis seemed to believe that the American presence would suddenly make all things possible that had previously been impossible. There was talk on the streets that overnight Iraq was going to become like Dubai and then even New York or London. The liberation from Saddam's regime, combined with a little contact with the outside world, made the Iraqis joyful, full of hope and love for the Americans who were going to bring all these miracles to them. It reminded me in some ways of early post-war Japan.

I saw that this perception of things was completely unrealistic. Partly as a result of the Baath Party's doctrine of socialism, any private entrepreneurial initiative had been completely leached out of Iraqis. Partly also, despite Saddam's secularism, the Arabic and Islamic throw-away line, *Inshallah* ("if Allah wills it"), was a perpetual statement that individuals really had no influence on the events of their own lives, much less on the country in which they lived. It was common—this blaming everything on God; and combined with the socialism, it was a fatal ingredient that continues to cause problems even today. I was constantly frustrated by the difficulty of motivating my own people, the Assyrians, into taking any initiatives to change their lives. As many of the Americans who really wanted the Iraqis to succeed with a new regime, I kept thinking that the Iraqis were simply lazy. When I yet again complained to an Assyrian relative how everybody just seemed to be waiting for someone else to come in and change things, he gently told me, "Amir, you have to realize what Saddam has done to us for 40 years. To be honest, we should all collectively be in mental hospitals. Saddam destroyed our souls. We know what the Americans are doing. They are right, and we are doing our best. But it is going to take time for us to believe again. We cannot change overnight. We need time."

The American troops who had entered Iraq full of enthusiasm and idealism wanted to see Iraq really turn into a prosperous, self-confident country as soon as possible. But because so many Iraqis relapsed into a sort of mood of fate-controls-everything, the Americans felt they were hitting their heads against a wall trying to stir up Iraqis to show initiative.

Despite obvious signs of progress in transforming Iraq displayed at the daily briefings in those early months after liberation, I was becoming worried by what I saw going on with the Assyrians. Out of a misplaced—at least I thought so—eagerness to show that they wanted the Muslims of Iraq—predominantly Shiites, of course—to succeed after so many years of Saddam's enforced secularism, the Americans seemed to be leaning heavily towards Iraqi Muslims. The Assyrians kept telling me that they felt themselves cut out of the process of restoring normal life in Iraq. It was apparent to all of us that the officialdom, in particular the UN, out of a desire to avoid the slightest suspicion of favoring fellow-Christians, was in fact tending to ignore the concerns of the Christians. The Americans at the top of the chain of command appeared to be palpably naïve. When I met one day with General Garner to explain this problem, he was frankly dismissive that there was a problem. "I just met with the Christian leaders," he said. "They told me that everything was all right."

"General Garner," I said, "thank you for your comments. May I ask if anyone else was in the room?"

He pondered the question for a few moments.

"Yes," he said, "there were some Iraqi officials."

"General Garner, did not you notice the way they were looking at the Christians? Do you recall what we Assyrians call 'the look'? That is the way that Iraqi officials convey to Christians the idea that they will be in trouble if they say anything critical of their situation."He looked at me with a slow expression of comprehending what he had just seen. Essentially, the Assyrian Christians with whom he had been meeting had been intimidated into mouthing complaisant platitudes by the presence in the room of Iraqi Muslim officials. But Garner's days were already numbered. He had been regarded as a natural choice by the Bush administration at the beginning of the post-combat administration of Iraq, given his earlier role in liaising with anti-Saddam Kurds in the north. In fact, the current president, Jalal Talibani, had worked closely with him. General Garner's initial job had been described to him by American officials as the task of developing and implementing plans to assist the Iraqis in learning how to govern themselves and reconstruct the country once Saddam Hussein was deposed. But it didn't work out that way.

Garner began organizing reconstruction efforts in March 2003—before the invasion was complete—with plans aiming for Iraqis to hold elections within 90 days and for the US to quickly pull troops out of the cities to a desert base. Jalal Talibani, a member of Jay Garner's staff in Kuwait before the war, was consulted on several occasions to help the US select a liberal Iraqi government. This would be the first government of democratic politicians to exist in Iraq. In an interview with *TIME* magazine, Garner stated that "as in any totalitarian regime, there were many people who needed to join the Baath Party in order to get ahead in their careers. We don't have a problem with most of them. But we do have a problem with those who were part of the thug mechanism under Saddam. Once the US identifies those in the second group, we will get rid of them." He was right. Many of my own relatives had been forced to join the Baath Party. If you were a teacher or any kind of government worker, you were required to be a member of the party. The party was large and very few had joined it by choice, which proved to be a huge weakness.

On April 15, 2003, General Garner called a conference in the city of Nasiriyah where he, along with 100 Iraqis, discussed the future of Iraq. Garner called a follow-up meeting of Iraqis on April 28, 2003. About 250 Iraqis attended this meeting, and seven of these Iraqis were selected personally by General Garner as the core leaders of the new Iraqi government: Masood Barzani, like Talibani, a Kurd, but from a rival Kurdish group, the Kudistan Democratic Party, was part of the team. The Shia figure Abdul Aziz Al Hakim was appointed as the leader of the Supreme Assembly for Islamic Revolution in Iraq. Ahmad Chalabi, a Shia Iraqi believed by many to have influenced the US administration assertion that Iraq had WMD (weapons of mass destruction) was chosen to represent the Iraqi National Congress, and Ayad Allawi was appointed as the leader of the Iraqi National Accord. Ibrahim al-Jaafari and Adnan al-Pachachi, the only Sunni, were also appointed.

Once the leaders were selected, a plan to hold elections in Iraq, where members would be elected, began on May 6, 2003, and ended on November 14, 2003, when the plan was abandoned. General Garner had wanted to have elections held within 90 days of the liberation of Iraq, but he was replaced by a new American administrator of Iraq, Ambassador Paul Bremer, who took up his role as head of the Coalition Provisional Authority (CPA), a sort of American pro-consul, on May 11 2003. Though Bremer was not personally against Garner, his appointment came with the unstated understanding that he would reintroduce order to Iraq. Bremer was a career foreign service officer who had been ambassador to the Netherlands in 1983 and, after retiring from the US

Foreign Service in 1989, became managing director of Kissinger and Associates. Following Garner's dismissal, the Coalition Provisional Authority started planning for a return of sovereignty to the Iraqi people in June 2004. The man named by Bremer to lead the Iraqi interim authority had been initially chosen by General Garner. Ayad Allawi was a former Baathist of Shiite origin. Allawi had many assets. He came across as a tough guy, and early on after Saddam's ouster, had quelled a noisy disturbance in a Baghdad market by firing his pistol into the air. He was determinedly secular. Many Iraqis told me that they thought he might be the best hope for ensuring that Iraq post-liberation remained secular.

With the arrival of Bremer, however, some things in Baghdad began to change visibly. In general, I saw most of the Americans and foreigners connected with the post-liberation regime as falling into two categories. There were the "true believers" that the Iraqis were falling in love with every day, that they called "angels" in the mission, mostly US military personnel who worked hard and really tried to help ordinary Iraqis. But there were also American officials of a State Department background who tended to have a different view of things. They probably wanted to be seen as having a more nuanced view of Iraq's problems than that of their military-background compatriots.

There seemed to be a profusion of self-described "cultural advisors" hanging around, Arabs of British citizenship, I inferred, who seemed to want to preserve as much as possible of Islamic culture in the emergent new Iraqi policy. Several of them had pronouncedly British accents when they spoke English. I recall one day when there was a meeting in the Convention Center. This had become the venue of the Iraqi Assistance Center, a civil organization established by the US liberation authorities to respond to requests from ordinary Iraqis to redress civic grievances or to have their humanitarian needs met. From early in the morning when the lines would start to form to well after dark, Iraqis would come to get help with their daily lives, which the angels took care of marvelously. At a meeting in July of 2004 there was an expert on city charters who had been imported for the occasion from the US. He passed onto me and my Assyrian friends what he said was the draft document for Baghdad's city charter. It opened with what I thought was a very strange passage for a city charter, "In the name of Allah, the compassionate the merciful." I knew, of course, that this phrase is from the Koran and is often used at the beginning of formal Islamic addresses. I confronted the expert immediately. "What is going on here?" I asked. "You are one of the top US experts in city charters. Would you insert 'All hail to Jesus' or a similar phrase in a city charter in the US?"

"Of course not. It wouldn't be professional."

"Well, why on earth do you do it here?" I asked.

"Well, they told me that this is how it is done here."

I knew immediately what he was saying. No Iraqi, unless one with a deep religious agenda after years of secular education, would be caught dead beginning the reading aloud of a city charter with religious words similar to the ones he had written down. It occurred to me that someone—perhaps one of the British-accented "cultural advisors" who kept showing up out of the blue—had gotten to this city charter man. This became a pattern.

After a month in Baghdad following my arrival with the supplies brought in from Jordan, things were beginning to get better all-round. The insurgency hadn't yet started up seriously and some Assyrian friends of mine in the US asked me to come back to Washington to meet with the State Department and other officials. I decided to go.

It was June 10, 2003, and my friend Fred and his cousin Ashur took me to the airport. I had not been there before and I hadn't known what to expect now that the Americans were in charge of things. The "airport" consisted of a tiny room on the corner of the former Baghdad Airport. Checking passengers in was a young female US officer who cheerfully checked our names against a list she had in her laptop, took some pictures of me, and stamped the CPA insignia in my US passport—another angel.

Several Iraqis who were standing by seemed to be very touched by this. I was emotionally touched too. She was not only professional and efficient, but remarkably pleasant. I had grown up in Japan hating war and indeed bearing hostile feelings towards my own country. Now my heart was being strangely melted by the basic decency of so many of the ordinary Americans I saw at work in Iraq.

Often I would travel on one of the small buses that were operated by American contractors to take people to different locations inside the Green Zone, the 10-square-kilometer area of Iraq that included the American embassy, the Iraqi Foreign Ministry and Parliament and many offices of the American administration inside Baghdad. On one particular occasion I found myself sitting next to an American soldier, in a conversation I was to have dozens of times. "Why are you here?" I asked, in retrospect a little brusquely.

"Just doing my job, sir," he said with the slow smile of a man who was clearly on the point of exhaustion. "I just want the Iraqis (which he pronounced *aye-rackies*) to have what we have, sir." The remark went down deep within me. Part of my emotional response was due to my recollection of how Dad had described to me the goodness of the American GI's who had helped rebuild post-war Japan over half a century earlier.

There must have been thousands of Americans like this young man on the bus, ordinary enlisted men and women and officers, or reserves, who were actually doctors and teachers and from many other professions who had been called up to fill the shortages, who were touching the Iraqis with their sweetness, their caring, and consistently working for their good.

Yet the help the Americans were providing was not, however, merely meek and mild. One day I was walking through the Convention Center across from the Rasheed Hotel in the Green Zone, in central Baghdad. The Convention Center had been taken over by the Americans and had many offices where American military personnel were attempting to deal with the many challenges emerging in the governance of Iraq. I passed by a room which had its door open. A quiet, female voice was speaking English. I peeked in and discovered an American woman officer addressing a room filled with Iraqi men. They were noisy and were speaking with each other all at once.

"Be quiet!" she suddenly ordered. Amazingly, the room went completely silent. As she made her lecture points about setting up a national NGO network in Iraq, she had the Iraqis' attention. There was no more buzz of anarchic conversation. She couldn't have been more than 25. What struck me, and strangely touched me, was the fact that this twenty-something-year-old, a volunteer in her nation's military, was in a foreign country where women were second class and constantly abused, making it clear to a crowd of unruly men that she wanted them to pay attention because she was working in their best interests—another angel.

I found that I was now completely losing my former hostility to America and Americans. I was starting to like the Americans, especially watching them "naively" trying to do the best they could in a strange, dusty and hot foreign country. They just tried to do the best job they could under the circumstances. As the days turned into weeks and the first summer after the invasion came around, I along with Iraqis all over the country were falling in love with the thousands of dedicated and idealistic young American angels who were "doing their job" in this foreign country. It was only later that we were told the stories of what happened in so many households immediately after liberation. Just as it happened in Japan a generation earlier, the Iraqis had been told that the Americans would come in and rape and pillage. In a story that was repeated throughout the country, one of my relatives described to me what had happened. An American contingent was set up nearby their house. Afraid to go out, they all peeked from behind their curtains to see what the Americans were doing. They were repairing the roads and fixing the buildings that had been damaged. A couple times a day, the family would gather round to discuss what the Americans were doing. "It looks like they are doing good!" one of the members would say. The others would convince that person that it was part of a trick or ruse. But as they days began to pass, all that they could see was good that the Americans were doing. Finally, they decided to send one of the children out to see what kind of response they would get. The child came back loaded with and candy, food, towels, and other goods. The family decided that the Americans were in fact here to do good, and immediately opened their doors. The love affair began.

I had by now been in Iraq since April 17, 2003. I felt I needed to get out of the country and tell as many people as I could what my impressions of the situation were. My first stop was London. When I arrive there in the second week of June 2003, together with Assyrians living in the British capital, we helped organize the first demonstration to thank the US-led coalition for liberating Iraq. We held the demonstration—well, it was really an "appreciation" event—outside 10 Downing Street, the official residence of the British prime minister, at that time Tony Blair. Dozens of Assyrian Christians living in London gathered to show their gratitude for the liberation of Iraq. It was in London that a very strange relationship first began. One of the Assyrians took me to an area of London called Golders Green, which was one of the Jewish neighborhoods in London. He took me to a friend of his who ran what could only be termed a Jewish communications agency. We met with the person in charge who asked us a lot about the situation of Assyrians in Iraq. He said he would see "what he could do." For the first time, I was meeting people who could understand the situation Assyrian Christians were going through in Iraq because we shared much of the same history. The Jews understood what it meant to suffer, and were the first to listen and offer us concrete help. It was there that I also saw firsthand the power of that same Jewish network. Literally the next day following our meeting, we began to receive requests for interviews and did a dozen or more interviews on the BBC, ITN, and other news organizations. I had a simple message: Iraqis were thanking the world for having been liberated from the Saddam Hussein regime. We made it clear that what the world now needed to do was protect the Assyrian Christians. We were even able to display the Assyrian flag I had first shown on Fox News during the war itself in Amman. I must have conducted twenty interviews within just a few days. The Jews were the only ones who seemed to understand, and at the same time cared to help us to get our message out. Just before I left, we had a final meeting where we thanked them for all their hard work in getting us out. The president gave me an address to go to in New York. "We will let them know you are coming and they will take care of you just as we have here in London," he told me.

I then flew to New York. The address given was an office building in lower Manhattan. I climbed the stairs to the third floor. When I rang the bell, a kindly-looking lady opened it. She smiled broadly and said, "We have been waiting for you."

As I entered the apartment, which was cluttered with papers and the detritus of organization meetings, I began introducing myself to the people there. A pleasant-looking man sitting behind a desk looked at me closely and said, "You look terrible! Go and get some sleep and come back tomorrow! Susie, get this guy fixed up at the hotel."

For a brief moment I was stunned by it all. Who were these wonderful, kindly people, and why were they putting themselves out for me?

The man turned out to be Rabbi Joseph Postanik, Executive Vice Chairman of the New York Board of Rabbis. His synagogue was Congregation Beth Sinai in Brooklyn. He was a well-known figure in the New York Jewish community. He was probably in his late 50's or early 60's, energetic and charming. He hosted a weekly radio program on ABC. It dawned on me that I really must have looked "terrible," for when I checked into the hotel, on their dime, I realized that I was completely exhausted. When I awoke, rested and refreshed the next morning, I found that they had lined up back-to-back interviews with Fox News, the BBC, CNN, ABC, and all manner of other news organizations. I learned more about the group over the next few days. When I was invited to speak at Rabbi Potanik's synagogue, I was surprised to learn nearly half of the audience had come from Baghdad. I realized why they cared so much for the Assyrians:

they had been through unimaginable suffering themselves.

Rabbi Potasnik invited me to come on his weekly radio program on ABC. He certainly didn't hold back from what he wanted to say. "I don't understand the Christians," he said on air. "They care so much about Israel but for some reason they don't seem to care for their fellow Christians in the Middle East. Israel already is a country. We have an army and a home. I tell you, the best way for people to support Israel is for the Christians of the world to support their fellow Christians in the Middle East." Over the next few days, and with a hasty amount of catch-up reading, I learned that Christians and Jews had formed a sizeable minority of Iraq's population right up to the 1950's perhaps as much as 40 percent of Baghdad's population. Christians and Jews had provided the manpower for the professions and middle class businesses. In effect, the middle class of Iraq, and for that matter the whole of the Middle East, the people who ran the markets, the gas stations and the consumer economy, had not been the Arabs, for the most part. They had been Christians and Jews. But from a significant minority of Iraq—perhaps as high as 20 percent as late as the 1950's—this demographic group had been whittled down by persecution and emigration to fewer than 10 percent of Iraqis today. I heard from Iraqis and from Assyrians that one way to address the problem of Iraq would be to "restore the balance," in effect to make Iraq a peaceable, democratic and civilly tolerant enough place to attract back so many of those who had emigrated over the years.

I realized that, just as in many European countries, it is the Jews who have been the "canaries in the mine"; in Iraq and throughout the Middle East as a whole it is the Christians who are now the canaries. And in Iraq, it is the Assyrians who are the canaries. The very compound of the Assyrians in Baghdad after its liberation from Saddam Hussein had formerly been one of his security service's torture establishments. After gaining control of Baghdad, the Americans found the list of those who had been killed and tortured there on the premises.

After all the meetings in New York, I flew back to Washington and met with various American officials who were involved in trying to manage the minorities in Iraq. I was becoming more and more familiar with the problems that had beset my own people, the Assyrians, once Iraq's political structure began to shift, while also realizing who our real friends were.

Signature of Sadat in my Bible

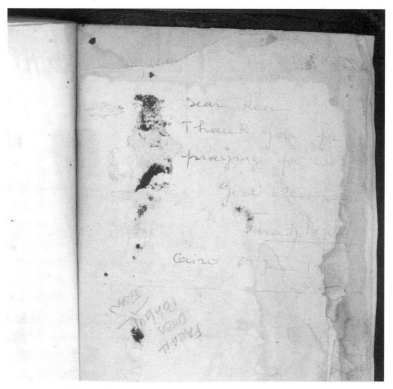

Signature of Sarah Pahlevi in my Bible

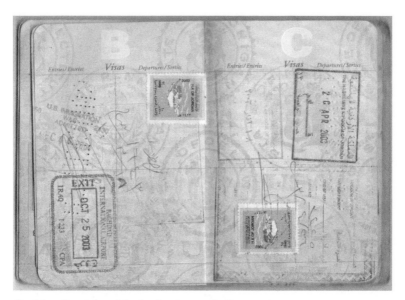

Coalition Provisional Authority Stamp in Passport

Coalition Provisional Authority Visa Stamp

Proclamation to the People of Iraq

I, Lieutenant General David McKiernan, Commander of all Coalition Ground Forces in Iraq, affirm to the citizens of Iraq the Coalition's commitment to restoring security, stability and rapidly repairing Iraq's damaged infrastructure. As the head authority in Iraq, I call for the immediate cessation of all criminal activity to include acts of reprisal, looting, and attacks on Coalition forces. Those who commit criminal acts, will be apprehended and be subject to criminal prosecution. I expect the support and assistance of the proud people of Iraq to restore stability to Iraq. To this end, I charge the citizens of Iraq to immediately return to work. Citizens who have served in leadership positions must identify themselves to Coalition forces to assist in the building of a new Iraqi government.

The Coalition, and the Coalition alone, retains absolute authority within Iraq. The Coalition will remain in control until it transfers its authority to a new firmly established and internationally recognized Iraqi Government. Individuals or organizations may not claim control of property, civil institutions or represent themselves as civil or military authorities without the explicit endorsement of the Coalition. Furthermore, the wearing of any distinguishing uniforms denoting a position of civil or military authority, specific group or organization is not authorized unless sanctioned by the Coalition. Likewise no one is authorized to speak as my representative or for Coalition forces. Those choosing to represent themselves in this manner will be considered a disruption to the stability of Iraq and treated as criminals. Additionally, all checkpoints and traffic control points, both established and planned, are not authorized unless directed and supervised by Coalition forces.

Together the noble people of Iraq and the Coalition will endeavor to reestablish a viable nation state and a model of success to the international community.

David D. McKiernan
Lieutenant General, United States

A poster drawn up by Gen. David McKiernan "Proclamation to The People of Iraq"

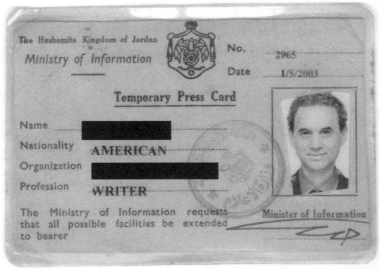

Author's Iraqi press card

Meeting with Prime Minister Maliki

Meeting with Iraq's president Jalal Talibani in New York, October 2008

Meeting with Richard Armitage

Iraqi Foreign Minister Hoshiyar Zebari with author

Papers dropped over Baghdad

Saddam Husein Iraqi Visa

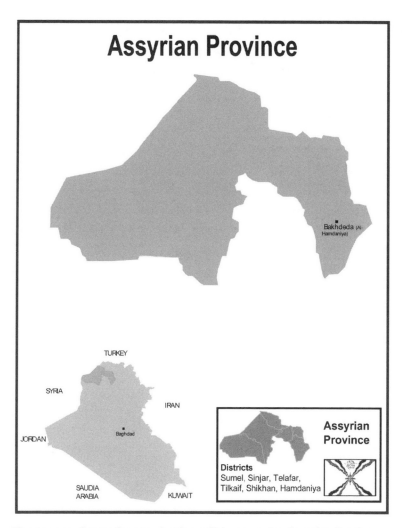

The proposed area they are hoping will become the Assyrian Province.

ID CARD NUMBER: 11656
ADDITIONAL INFORMATION

Date of Birth: 02 MAR 1957
Place of Birth: TOKYO, JAPAN
Height: 5'11"
Weight: 170 LBS
Hair Color: BLONDE
Eye Color: BROWN
Passport Number: 035544015
Passport Country: USA
Passport Expiration: 31 AUG 2005

This card has been issued by
The Coalition Press Information Center (CPIC)
for media accreditation purposes only.
For further information call

914-360-5089 (COMM) 318-239-0272 **(DSN)**
302-550-2522 (DNVT) 318-836-1123 **(DSN)**

This card is the property of the United States Government
and must be openly displayed. If found, return to the nearest
US Military Installation or Embassy

Author's Press ID

CHAPTER SEVEN

MY RETURN

WHEN I RETURNED to Baghdad after my London and American foray in the spring of 2003, it was by now August. Many things had changed in the weeks I had been away. ORHA, of course, originally run by General Garner, had now long gone and the presiding authority in Baghdad was the Coalition Provisional Authority, the CPA. The daily briefings in Saddam's palace were still going on and many Iraqis seemed to be optimistic. The "can-do" spirit of the Americans was certainly having some impact on the Iraqis with whom they came into contact. I couldn't help noticing that the Iraqis I daily associated with were much better educated than the Americans who were now running their government. "Uneducated kids!" the Iraqis would often mumble to me. But then they would add, "But they are so wonderful and full of hope." They loved and admired them all the same.

In Baghdad things were changing fast. Our satellite phones

were continuing to be used. In fact, the only phone service was that provided by Thuraya Satellite, and ordinary phone calls made through them—though not through ours, of course—cost up to $5 a minute. This was especially true in downtown Baghdad. The Japanese volunteers had long since delivered all the mail with which they had been entrusted in Amman. Now they set up shop in Fidrous Square in central Baghdad, opening a "post office" for Iraqis to come to if they wanted international delivery to their relatives outside Iraq. We were still practically running the only "post office" and "telephone service" in Iraq!

A flood of foreign cars had poured into Baghdad and the city streets were becoming clogged by them. Traffic was now a major problem. Iraqis were complaining daily about the terrible traffic.

"We used to go in ten minutes. Now it takes an hour!" they would say. I tried to explain to them that traffic meant progress, but they didn't understand. So I asked them, "Well, could you own a car under Saddam?" and of course they would rather bashfully answer, "No." I explained to them that now everybody could own a car. Traffic was a part of every major city.

Finally the Internet came to Baghdad. One location where it was available opened up in a private home in the Al Mansour district of Baghdad. In practice, this meant that access was limited to foreign reporters and workers for Non-Government Organizations (NGO's). I recalled how I had tried to send an email in Saddam's time from the UN headquarters and over and over found the words, "site blocked." In addition, the UN had its headquarters at the Canal Hotel in Baghdad. Aside from the Al Mansour location, it was one of the few places one could also get online in Baghdad. Not surprisingly, a large number of people began to hang out at the Canal Hotel.

It was August 22, 2003. I had planned to meet up with my

Assyrian relative, Fred, so that he could drive me to the Canal Hotel and I could get online. We planned to go at 4:00 p.m., which was when the Internet connection was strongest. Today, however, Fred showed up half an hour late. I started screaming at him. "What's wrong with you, how come you're late?" I shouted. Fred tried to explain how bad the traffic had been that day, but I didn't let up. As we set off for the Canal Hotel, we found that the traffic was blocked. As we neared the area, we could see in the distance what remained of the Canal Hotel. It had been bombed and just at 4:00 p.m., when we would have been there

We stopped the car and I turned to Fred and apologized profusely. Fred had saved my life. One of the UN officials killed in the blast was Sergio Vieira de Mellow, the UN High Commissioner for Human Rights. In fact, the bomb had specifically been positioned to destroy his office. The reason given for the murder of this distinguished diplomat by Iraq's Al Qaeda chieftain Al Zarqawi was that he had helped East Timor, a predominantly Christian community, become independent from Muslim Indonesia. Zarqawi's rationale was that no minority, least of all Christians, had the right to become independent from "Muslim lands."

Three months after the UN bombing there was an incident near the airport that indicated the beginning of some real problems. A DHL cargo plane was taking off from Baghdad airport when it was shot at by someone firing either a rifle or a machine gun. There was no damage. Symbolically, however, it marked the dashing of the hopes of Iraqis who had dreamed just a few weeks earlier that their capital city would be connected to other major capitals of the world. Insurance companies had underwritten the value of all planes flying into Iraq before this incident. As naïve as it sounds, hope was in the air and we along with the Iraqis truly believed that newly liberated Iraq was going to become like Dubai with daily flights anywhere in the world. The DHL shooting symbolically crashed that dream for many of us. Now they were not willing to insure most incoming flights. In fact, well into 2009, passenger-carrying flights into Baghdad were airliners that had no markings at all and were painted completely white. There were no airline logs, and the crews were a wild-west hodge-podge of Russians, South Africans and vaguely Balkan nationalities. The Russian pilots had a reputation for being "cowboys," willing to push the envelope of aircraft performance in order to make a cargo or passenger delivery. And the Russian cabin crew would sometimes make one nostalgic for the Soviet era of Aeroflot.

I recall a rather hair-raising takeoff from Baghdad my first flight in June 2003. The plane had performed the routine "Baghdad swing," climbing up in tight circles instead of making a normal, straight-out departure in order to not be targeted by heat-seeking missiles. As the plane continued to bank in its spiraling ascent, the wing opposite the direction of the bank suddenly dipped down. "We've been hit!" someone shouted from a seat a few rows behind me. Actually, we hadn't been, but we'd experienced a near-miss by a RPG (rocket-propelled grenade) fired at the plane. Reddish smoke in the air marked the close passage by our wing of the projectile. When the plane touched down at its destination in Amman, Jordan, everybody heaved a sigh of relief and thanks to God for protecting us. Once again, I had almost been killed.

On the ground in Iraq the insurgency was coming into being. The city had hitherto been easy to get around. Now it was overcrowded with traffic and there were some really dangerous insurgents who had infiltrated their way into town. I learned this the hard way when driving down the crazily crowded Palestine

Street. Fred was driving me to the Palestine Hotel in downtown Baghdad. We had been nervous about the bombing and locked the doors and windows front and back, despite the heat. Suddenly, I looked out on the passenger's side and saw a gun-barrel pointed directly at me. It was touching the windshield. Then what happened was so rapid I can hardly reconstruct the sequence of events. Somehow, the would-be kidnappers—for that is what they were—managed to open the passenger door of the car, grab me by the arm, and hurl me face down in the street. Now my legs were in the car and the barrel was pointed directly at my head.

My first and immediate thought was that this was the end of my life. To use Christian jargon, I was "going home"—I was about to die. In that instant of realization how close to death I was I had the momentary satisfaction of realizing that I had at least died in a good cause, trying to help my people, the Assyrian people. But Fred had instantly gotten out of the car on his side when he saw the two men trying to kidnap me and he started shouting something at them in Arabic. For no reason I could at that moment understand, whatever he said spooked them completely. The man hesitated, then pulled his gun away from the back of my head. Then he and his comrade took off by foot as fast as they could.

Fred was panting with fear, as I was, his face paler than a sheet.

"What did you say to them?" I asked.

"I told them that you were a man of God and that if they killed you, God would be their enemy. That sort of talk is the only thing that works with them."

I wondered. Though Fred was surely telling the truth when he described his words, I thought I must have had some sort of divine protection to have escaped their clutches. For the second time in a month Fred had saved my life. The daily briefings by the US authorities were continuing at Saddam's palace, now the headquarters of the Coalition Provisional Authority. After one of the daily briefings a staffer invited several journalists to one of Saddam's former personal rooms in the palace. It was now being used as an exercise center for American military units. At a table where we sat down, we noticed a whole array of food dishes that had been carefully preserved in what looked like Saran Wrap. Fred saw me looking quizzically at it all and then explained.

"That was Saddam's food," he said. "He lived in constant fear that he might be poisoned and ordered his food, before he ate it, to be covered in plastic wrap to prevent anyone from tampering with it after it had been prepared. Then the Assyrian taster would taste the food first to make sure it wasn't poisoned." This shows the love that the Iraqis have towards for the Assyrians, and the trust they place in them, because they know they are Christians and that they can be trusted. I couldn't help reflecting on this vestige of an evil, totalitarian dictatorship, and contrast it with the young men and women, American service personnel, who were doing their best, as they firmly believed—and I certainly did, too—to restore Iraq to a "normal," civilized community.

I had been staying at the Assyrian church in downtown Baghdad where we had initially stayed after my first return to Iraq following the American invasion. At the suggestion of the Assyrians on my return from one of my trips out of the country, I had moved to another church building, located in between the Iranian embassy and the newly formed Green Zone that had originally been called Saddam City. The term "Green Zone" referred to the green signs that were placed in front of safe areas, as opposed to red signs signifying danger, or yellow signs signifying caution. In an interesting twist, as they were closing part of the Green Zone, I was given permission to take one of the actual "green" signs. As far as I know I possess the only Green Zone sign that stood at the Rasheed Gate.

The church building could not have been more appropriately placed, with the Americans on the right and the Iranians on the left, who were fighting for power in liberated Iraq. One Sunday morning when I was preparing to go to church, the entire building where I was staying shook violently. Then, a fraction of a second later, there was a massive boom.

Since I had grown up in Japan, I was used to earthquakes, but this was different. Fred and I immediately climbed to the flat roof of the building on which Iraqis often sleep in the hot summer months. The building where I was staying had a unique location in Baghdad. It was on the edge of the Green Zone, the central area of Baghdad in which the US embassy, the major American military headquarters, and the offices of the most important Iraqi government agencies were located. The Green Zone had become much harder to enter following the UN headquarters bombing. As we looked from the top of the building towards the Green Zone I noticed flames coming from the entrance of the Green Zone. Soon, an American tank took up a position on the church lawn. Across the street was a CNN crew with a reporter I knew doing a live shot in front of us.

This was the first bombing we were seeing firsthand and it had taken place just next to where we were staying. I thought we should stay inside the building until it was clear what had happened, but Father Yeshua, ever the disciplined Assyrian Christian, insisted that we go to church as usual. He explained his reasoning this way, "If we didn't go to church every time something happened, we would never go." Actually, at this point in time the Assyrians and the Iraqis were generally upbeat about what was happening in Iraq. The Assyrians were happy that one of their own, Yonaddam Kanna, had been appointed by Bremer to the "Governing Council," Iraq's first stab at a post-invasion government. I had, of course, first met Kanna in London at the Iraqi conference in November 2002.

The CPA had become pretty well-organized under the new Bremer regime – whatever my subsequent misgivings about the direction I thought Bremer was taking Iraq in, and there was a press office at the Convention Center. Press briefings were held daily, as they had been soon after the American headquarters was set up. I would attend whenever I could and try to ensure that a case was being made for the protection of the Assyrians. The press conferences ran like clockwork. I couldn't help admiring the efficiency and goodwill of the young American servicemen and women who ensured everything worked properly. I had the impression that ordinary Iraqis, journalists and other observers who had contact with the Iraqi personnel running the convention center were very favorably impressed with what they saw. Several times, either from an Iraqi who spoke English or through Fred's translation from Arabic, I would hear a comment like, "Oh, the Americans are so good." The word "good" implied not only well-organized and efficient, but, in my view more importantly, decent and well-disposed to Iraqis.

Yet I couldn't help noticing something else going on. Among the crowd of foreign reporters and NGO representatives accredited to cover the early months of the American presence in Baghdad there were several people who seemed really hostile to what the US was trying to do. Several Iraqis commented to me about this phenomenon. Fred referred to such people, like many of the Iraqis did, as "the anti-American Americans," and I couldn't help understanding why he was using this term. We were all struck by how much animosity was openly expressed by many of these people toward President George Bush and to the American military establishment. We had noticed this several times when forming a line with other foreigners and Iraqis to get into the Green Zone. You'd hear some really offensive jokes and other comments leveled at the US presence in Iraq by some of the foreigners. I noticed several reporters, usually Americans, attempting to provoke young American servicemen guarding the Green Zone into lashing out and actually hitting the journalists. These young men, often marines, had to endure security duty for hours at a time in the hot sun, but they would endure mockery and criticism from the critical American reporters and observers, the anti-American Americans. To some of them, it seemed to be a point of honor to claim that an American guard had physically reacted to their taunts. "I got a young marine to hit me yesterday," was one comment I recall overhearing in the line to enter the Green Zone.

I'm afraid I began to feel like many ordinary Americans who perceive American reporters as viscerally hostile to American interests overseas, and particularly hostile to any conservative American administration in the White House. I couldn't help thinking that some of these reporters wanted to report the situation on the ground in Iraq as negatively as possible. The CPA was certainly working hard to attempt to restore normalcy to the Iraqi infrastructure and economy. Despite complaints—no doubt in some cases justified—from many Iraqis that progress was not fast enough, schools *were* being built, water supply *was* being increased, and possibly most remarkable of all, electricity *was* becoming more reliable and accessible.

The original electric grid in Iraq had been built by the British in the 1950s. In the 1980s, Saddam Hussein set up his own personal electric grid where, first, all electricity went to Hussein's modern network that supplied all of his palaces and facilities. Then, what remained was supplied to Baghdad. If there was anything left, and often there wasn't, it went to the rest of the country. With liberation, military contractors began the tedious process of trying to join the two grids—Saddam's and the country's. This was no small task. One was modern and the other, over 50 years old. What resulted as the two systems were merged was the equal flow of electricity for the first time. What this did, though, was necessarily decrease electricity in Baghdad, simply because it was going to areas outside for the first time in history.

Another thing happened: with freedom for the first time, Iraqis could have cell phones, computers, and air conditioners. Overnight it was going from the 1960s to the 21st century, and the use of electricity skyrocketed. While the US Army Corps of Engineers built electric power plant after electric power plant, the demand for electricity continued to increase resulting ironically in a decrease in power in Baghdad, while the overall power was growing rapidly.

I flew out by helicopter to one of the first newly built electric power plants with the Electricity Minister, a friend of Barack Obama's from Chicago. There was great excitement by those who saw the dramatic developments, but the US failed to explain the situation to the public because as we discussed earlier, the Iranians were the only ones who were broadcasting news. The Americans could not explain to the public that power had in fact increased. The Iraqis in Baghdad saw their electricity drop from 12 hours a day to less than six. Meanwhile, the daily Iranian broadcast said the Americans were stealing Iraqis' oil and electricity.

Something else that was happening was the traffic. It had been impossible to own a car in Saddam's Iraq. Overnight the border disappeared and instantly every used and available new car was brought from Jordan. Forty years of pent-up need was being pro-vided in days and weeks. Naturally, a system that had operated with literally no private cars was not prepared to handle the tens of thousands of cars crossing the border uninhibited. These were good problems, yet the long mix of Islamic socialism had cre-ated immature and defeatist people completely dependent on the government with no personal initiative, resulting in an attitude that instantly turned on the system when things didn't go right.

Most perplexing to Iraqis—those who weren't actual sup-porters of the insurgency—was the venom so often expressed towards President Bush, and in a larger sense, to America itself.

I recall one remarkable press conference when the Iraqi For-eign Minister, Hoshor Zebari, was making some points about Iraq's domestic and international situation. An American jour-nalist stood up and said—I paraphrase his remarks, not having recorded the question verbatim—"First, I would like to apolo-gize to you for the terrible occupation my country has imposed on Iraq without finding any weapons of mass destruction. I—"

Rather brusquely, Zebari slammed his hand on the podium in a room filled with almost 200 people. "You are an Ameri-can," he said. "What is wrong with you? What occupation? We were liberated from a terrible regime. How dare you use a word like 'occupation'! As regards the weapons of mass destruction, which ones would you like to know about? Those that weren't trucked into Syria? Those that are buried in the desert? Those that were spirited away to Iran? You ought to be ashamed of yourself." As we shall see later, Zebari was not making up what many Iraqis had known about the WMD. (Karl Rove later ad-dresses this in his book *Courage and Consequences: My Life as a Conservative in the Fight.* More recently, retired US Army Major General Paul Vallely states that he has confirmation that

Syrian forces have used chemical weapons against rebel forces and civilians that are likely stockpiles received from Iraq prior to the US-led invasion).

The silence in the room was deafening. Many reporters shifted uneasily in their chairs, probably feeling that the foreign minister had rebuked them implicitly as well. I thought it was a striking example of how out of touch some American reporters were with an emerging segment of Iraqi political thinking. I think some of the Iraqis in the room were as amazed as the foreign minister had been at the dark sentiment of hostility to the US, or at least to American policy towards Iraq expressed by the reporter, once again, one of the anti- American Americans.

A similar incident took place at another press conference, this time in the United States. Iraqi ambassador to the US Samir Sumaid'ie was speaking to journalists in Washington, DC, in 2005. Not long before the press conference, a notorious incident had occurred involving US Marines in the Iraqi town of Haditha. I was in Washington, DC, at the time. As someone who had met Sumaid'ie on several previous occasions, I wanted to know how he was going to handle himself. Once again, an American reporter, I think from one of the three main American newsmagazines, stood up and said the following—I am paraphrasing—"Mr. Ambassador, I want to present to you my deepest apologies for the terrible killings in Haditha." It was as if the reporter felt that the entire US had been implicated by the mishap and he, an American reporter, wanted to apologize for it.

The reporter had barely gotten the sentence out of his mouth before Sumaid'ie looked agitated and angry, stopping him.

"Sir," he said, "You are an American, aren't you? Do you know where Haditha even is? Do you know who lives in Haditha? We Iraqis know Haditha. Everyone living in Haditha is either a terrorist, a relative of a terrorist, or a friend of a terrorist. We know the Americans. They don't go into people's homes and shoot them up. What's wrong with you? The people of Haditha should be grateful that it wasn't the Iraqi forces that entered the town. If they had been Iraqi forces, there would have been shooting." Once again, the anti-American Americans struck.

Just as had happened at the Foreign Minister's press conference earlier, there was an embarrassed silence. The reporter had probably anticipated an indignant display of displeasure at American actions. But he was disappointed. Once again, it was an Iraqi who had stood up for the American presence in Iraq... to an American.

We were constantly facing this extremely strange situation where the Iraqis were saying, "We want to be like you!" For all their lives they had dreamed of America. Now they were meeting some of the Americans, living and working with them, and suddenly learning the Americans didn't seem to like their own country.

The other incident that kept coming up was Abu Ghraib. The outside world looked at it as an excuse to say how terrible the Americans were acting towards Iraq and towards Iraqis. However, within Iraq, the reaction was dramatically different. Like the DHL shooting had squashed the dreams of Iraq becoming the next Dubai, Abu Ghraib sent shudders down the Iraqis' spines because their view of it was that the Americans did not have what it took to combat evil in the country. One relative, whom I shall call William, a well-built, handsome man who had served in the Iraqi army but had also fallen into terrible disfavor with Saddam Hussein, came up to me shortly after the Abu Ghraib story broke with what I thought was a strange expression on his face. In fact, he was grinning. I had known about his courageous display of opposition to the Saddam regime and had heard something about his mistreatment by Saddam's goons.

"Do you know the real Abu Ghrabi?" he said. "I do. I was in Abu Ghraib. I was thrown into Abu Ghraib for being associated with a banned group of Assyrians. Every day after lunch, as though making it routine, they would come into our cells and beat us. On Sunday mornings they would hang people." Then he pulled up his shirt and pant legs. He wanted me to see the multiple cigarette burns and other scars he had acquired as an inmate in Saddam's Abu Ghraib. His head was conspicuous for there was a huge gash across his forehead, another emblem of membership in the involuntary Abu Ghraib club.

"The real Abu Ghraib, the one under Saddam, was terrible," he went on. "It really makes me sad to see the way people outside of Iraq are complaining about what the Americans are doing at Abu Ghraib. If the Americans are too tender to rough up these thugs they have under their control, there is little chance the Americans will succeed. The people the Americans are holding in Abu Ghraib are the worst of the worst." In effect, this brave Assyrian—the one I had dubbed Braveheart in my mind—doubted the Americans would have the internal fortitude, the spine, to make their foray into Iraq work, an opinion shared by many Iraqis. I was reminded of what Yonaddam Kana had said to me very soon after I had returned once Saddam had been overthrown. He knew the Americans, he said. They wouldn't be staying long.

From the perspective of the Assyrians, and indeed from that of all Iraqis who had suffered under Saddam, keep in mind that nearly one million people had been killed either directly or indirectly by Saddam Hussein, the regime that the Americans had displaced was pure evil. Almost every Iraqi family had some family member who had run afoul of Saddam's thugs or torturers. Almost every Iraqi home had one or more pictures on the wall of a family member who had been killed by Saddam. They held—and they constantly reminded me of this—that the evil that had been represented by the Saddam regime, and now by the Islamists and insurgents who were doing their best to destabilize Iraq, would not be treated with, negotiated with, much less compromised with. This form of evil simply had to be defeated.

The Abu Ghraib incident, in contrast to the way it was reported to the world, sent a shiver of fear down the Iraqis. Many of them were well aware of the wickedness of some of the insurgents being held in Abu Ghraib, and some of these insurgents being held in Abu Ghraib were supporters of Sadam Hussein who had so oppressed them. Some Iraqis told me that the only thing that would change the minds of the miscreants being held at Abu Ghraib would be to beat them within an inch of their lives. Only then, some of my Iraqi friends told me, would the prisoners being held by the Americans begin to see how they had been influenced by the regime of Saddam. I didn't have the guts to share this sentiment, but the fact is that some Iraqis couldn't understand why the Americans wouldn't be really tough on the insurgents. In fact, they became quite fearful in their discussions about it with me. Perhaps, they said, America didn't have the spine to fight against these evil people and defeat them. Were the Americans, they asked, too "soft" to do what needed to be done in Iraq? The Iraqis were worried.

That brings me back to the Americans in Iraq whom my Assyrian friends had dubbed the "anti-American Americans." Everyone in Iraq was on tenterhooks waiting for the significant date of July 28, 2004, when the Americans handed over Iraq sovereignty to Prime Minister Allawi, whose secretary was one of my relatives. I along with most Iraqis felt it was too soon. I wrote a piece for United Press International called "June is too Soon" arguing that there had not been enough time to set up the institutions needed, and the rush to hand over power would cause huge problems, which proved to be true.

On the morning of the auspicious date scores of journalists, NGO representatives and observers, and others were gathered in a basement room of the press room in the Convention Center. Actually, the Iraqi authorities had gone through a charade of driving US reporters around in buses supposedly in order that we wouldn't know where the meeting was going to be held.

Some of the faces among the reporters chronically critical of the White House—remember, this was the *Bush* White House— or simply antagonistic to what the Americans were trying to do in Iraq, were gleeful that what was about to happen amounted to a new day for Iraq, a day in which the interfering Americans would be forced into the background. Some of them, in snatches of conversation I overhead around the room, seemed to think that ordinary Iraqis would be letting off firecrackers, firing rifles into the air and dancing in the streets at the changeover.

I knew better. All my Assyrian friends had watched glumly as the Americans prepared to take a back-seat in the governance of Iraq. As far as they were concerned, the longer the Americans stayed, the better for them. Who knew what kind of Iraqi government might emerge once the dust had settled?

I myself had written some commentaries and articles that were carried on a website viewed by many worldwide Assyrians and on other websites indicating I thought it was far too soon to end the role of the CPA barely more than a year after the Americans had first arrived.

I wrote at the time that I thought there were three reasons why the handover over of sovereignty should not take place at the time as it had been announced, at the end of June 2004. First of all, it was just too soon. After thirty-five years of a reign of terror, it was too much to expect that the basics of good government could be put together in Iraq in a little over a year. In Japan after World War II it took seven years for the militarist regime to be replaced by a solid, functioning democratic system. Second, I thought it absurd that the UN would now be looked to as an institution to fill the responsibilities of the US. My impression of the attitude of Iraqis to the UN was that it was both hated and despised. Iraqis had watched how, during the time of Sadaam Hussein, instead of supporting them, the UN not only did not stand up to Sadaam Hussein, but it presided over an "Oil for Food" that enriched a handful of Iraqis – and according to many observers, some UN officials – while it did nothing to help ordinary Iraqis. I agreed with the Iraqis I had talked to that the UN simply didn't have the means or the integrity to serve as a training wheel for the emergent Iraqi government. Third, I had written that, with such a short and arbitrary deadline, the vast majority of Iraqis who supported the changes that had been accomplished by the Americans—the "silent majority" in fact— would be too intimidated after the hand-over to speak out or act. Simply put, I had written, if anyone outwardly expressed approval for the changes the Americans were achieving in Iraq, once power was no longer with the Americans, he or she would quite possibly be targeted for murder. I thought and had written that Iraq's "silent majority" was precisely the "engine of growth" that needed to be engaged in the country's progress so that it could move further forwards. A member of the Iraqi Governing Council, my Assyrian friend called Yonadem Kanna, had toured the United States a few weeks earlier and insisted that most of the Iraqis were in fact very grateful for their liberation by the Americans and for the continuing presence of American forces.

But now, here we all were on the morning of June 28, awaiting the signing of the hand-over documents. The actual ceremony had been scheduled for 10.15 a.m. I began to feel a little uncomfortable, and at first I wasn't sure why. Then I realized that in the press conference room itself were faces I hadn't seen around for a long time, in fact since Saddam's time. As if from nowhere, some of the minders I recognized from my very first arrival in Iraq in January 2003 had somehow showed up again.

Among many reporters, the atmosphere of distaste for the US government was palpable to me. The prevailing mood among reporters was that the Americans had now been put in their place, and the anti American-Americans were excited.

But what was happening in the center of the room, where the newly emergent Iraqi regime was flexing its muscles, didn't at all suggest that. An Iraqi government spokesman approached the microphone and in one of the first acts of the new government, called out, "BBC, *Los Angeles Times*," he said, "Come up here."

I was only feet from the podium and I watched with fascination and a certain anticipation of humor as the Iraqi took out of his briefcase two pieces of paper that seemed to be copies of news stories the new Iraqi authorities had been monitoring.

"I don't like these," said the Iraqi, waving the pieces of paper disdainfully. "Change them." He then threw, yes threw, the copies of their stories at the reporters who had, with some surprise, come to the podium in response to his orders.

I was close enough to them to talk directly to them as they scrambled around to pick up the pieces of paper that had fallen to the ground.

"Well," I said, hardly restraining a chuckle, "it looks like you got what you wanted. The new Iraqi government has been flexing its muscles, and the first order of the day is censorship!" Both men, who well knew that I had been a fierce champion of what the Americans were trying to do, scowled at me.

It was obvious by now that the delirious celebrations that some reporters had anticipated at the retreat of the Americans weren't taking place. No one was dancing in the streets or firing off bursts of AK-47 bullets into the air. Yet in the press room there was, on most faces I thought, clear disappointment. Where was all the celebrating that had been forecast by them? "What happened to all the dancing in the streets?" I asked a group of reporters who had been conspicuous in their prediction of Iraqi jubilation at the hand-over.

"Word hasn't gotten out yet," one answered. "It will come."

By mid-day, however, it was clear that Iraqis, in Baghdad at least, were not rejoicing at all in the change of sovereignty that had just occurred. In fact, later in the day, there was panic and some Iraqis came up to me with the question, "Are the Americans going to leave?"

No, they weren't, not quite yet. But I thought they had set in motion processes for which ordinary Iraqis would later pay a high price.

CHAPTER EIGHT

THE ISLAMIC REPUBLIC OF IRAQ?

IBEGAN TO NOTICE a very strange phenomenon: the "establishment," minus the military, seemed to have a distinct distaste for American values. This attitude was also reflected among reporters and NGO workers. After Ambassador Bremer had taken over the CPA, more and more State Department officials were seconded to the CPA to provide guidance for the transition to full Iraqi political control. The Iraqis kept saying that it seemed the new officialdom, in particular the UN advisors, were bending over backwards to not displease the emergent Islamic community in Iraq and that, in effect, some of them seemed to be "more Muslim than we are—we are not that religious—we just want to become a normal country. We just got rid of one totalitarian state in Saddam—we don't want to replace it with another, this time religious."

The officialdom could never seem to understand that the Iraqis wanted the same separation of Church and State that those designing their future enjoyed. They did not seem to understand that the Iraqis hated Saddam, but they hated even more being ruled by religious leaders. "We just want to be like you," was the simple refrain.

They certainly had no sympathy at all for the Assyrian Christian community that had suffered so much in Iraq nor any understanding of history that the Assyrians were the original people in Iraq. Most of them seemed to feel that, whereas there was a separation of church and state in the United States, it was inconceivable to live in the Middle East and not be a Muslim. But even though a sizable chunk of the Iraqi population of Iraq was technically Shiite Muslim, the Iraqis wanted a government that was secular: that is to say, they really didn't want the government to be "religious" itself. My impression was that the majority of ordinary Iraqis had no respect for their mullahs. I even heard some of them saying that they thought at best 5 percent were any good. One Iraqi woman said, "I'll give you a good example of how evil the mullahs are. The other day, one of the mullahs came to my house and started shouting at me, telling me the women needed to cover their heads. I threw sand at him to make him leave. That same afternoon, my daughter rushed into my house, panicking, because that same mullah had tried to grab her on her way home from school. This shows who they really are. They say one thing, and do another." She was hardly able to control her anger.

At the outset of the American presence in Iraq, US officials seemed energetic in saying that America was now the source of political authority in Iraq and that no alternative source would be tolerated. For example, a critical policy poster had been drawn up by Gen. David McKiernan, the commander of all allied ground forces in Iraq. The poster read in English and Arabic:

"Proclamation to the people of Iraq. I, Lieutenant General

David McKiernan, Commander of All Coalition Ground Forces in Iraq, affirm to all citizens of Iraq the coalition's commitment to restoring security, stability, and rapidly repairing Iraq's damaged infrastructure. As the local authority in Iraq, I call for the immediate cessation of all criminal activity to include acts of reprisal, looting, and attacks on coalition forces. Those who commit criminal acts will be apprehended and subject to criminal prosecution. I expect the support and resistance of the proud people of Iraq to restore stability to Iraq. To this end, I charge the citizens of Iraq to immediately return to work. Citizens who have served in leadership positions must identify themselves to coalition forces to assist in the building of a new Iraqi government. The coalition and the coalition alone retains absolute authority within Iraq. The coalition will remain in control until it transfers its authority to a new firmly established and internationally recognized Iraqi government. Individuals or organizations may not claim control of property, civil institutions or represent themselves as civil or military authorities without the explicit endorsement of the coalition. Furthermore the wearing of any distinguishing uniforms denoting a position of civil or military authority, specific group or organization, is not authorized unless sanctioned by the coalition. Likewise, no one is authorized to speak as my representative for the coalition forces. Those choosing to represent themselves in this manner will be considered a disruption to the stability of Iraq and treated as criminals. Additionally, all checkpoints and traffic control points both established and planned are not authorized unless directed and supervised by coalition forces. Together, the noble people of Iraq and the coalition will endeavor to re-establish a viable nation state and a model of success to the international community. David B. McKiernan, Lieutenant General, United States"

Given the relentlessly anti-American broadcasts in Arabic beamed into the country from Iran, the poster was of huge significance. We kept going to various representatives of the US administration in Baghdad and pointing out that many ordinary Iraqis didn't seem to know who was in charge or what was happening in the country. We said it was vital to get the poster's message broadly known throughout the country. "Don't worry," we were told, "this poster had been put up everywhere in Iraq."

I suspected that this wasn't the case at all. To verify the real situation, Fred and another Assyrian from the church, Minos, and I, drove out of Baghdad in April 2003 to Mosul, north of the Iraqi capital. Mosul, in fact, was near the location of the original Biblical city of Niniveh and to this day Iraqis refer to the surrounding area as Nineveh. To get there, we drove through, among other points, Saddam's hometown of Tikrit.

We didn't see the poster anywhere. None was visible in any town through which we drove from Baghdad to Mosul—they were supposed to be posted at every public space. After we left Mosul, we stayed for a couple days in Sarsink with Minos' family. One morning Fred said, "How would you like to see your hometown?" I was shocked that he was able to find it. We all got in the car and drove about twenty minutes away to the village of Mahoudi. Mahoudi was a classic example of what had happened to one of the largest Christian communities in the Middle East. While it had once been a thriving farming village, all that was left was rubble and what looked like five or six families. To add insult to injury, where the church once stood was a massive, ugly green mosque. It broke my heart to see the state of the village that my family came from, but then anger at the viciousness that not only destroyed the village, but built a huge mosque just to make a political point. I left Mahoudi that day with a heavy heart, but also with a firsthand understanding of why my grandparents had to leave in the dead of night.

On returning to Baghdad, we notified the authorities of what we had discovered, to wit, no poster. Later we discovered that the posters had never even left a Baghdad warehouse. Someone in the American bureaucracy in Baghdad had evidently sat on the order to distribute the poster nationwide. An anti-American American? Who knew. It was very discouraging. In listening informally to the conversation of many US officials in Iraq, I had the impression that many of them had no heart for what the US was trying to achieve in Iraq, and might have even wanted the American effort to fail altogether. There was a lot of discussion among some of these officials about job opportunities that might be coming up in the US bureaucracy in Washington, which seemed to be their main focus. After all, the elections of 2004 were fast approaching. It was simple—if Iraq went well, Bush would win and they would be out of a job. If Kerry won, they would have their coveted place in Washington. They didn't seem to care much about the Iraqis. In fact, they were usually isolated from them. They seemed to be there mainly to fluff up their resumes. The temptation to not push programs must have been tremendous. If I had been a Democrat with a politically-provided job in Iraq, I might have been tempted to overlook some vital task in the administration of the country. I would probably not want things happening inside Iraq to give the impression that US policy was being successful and influence the upcoming election.

Oddly enough, what seemed to endear many Iraqis to the Americans was not grandiose American visions of a transformed Middle East led by a peaceable, democratic Iraq. Rather, it seemed to be the host of small things the Americans did, practical things that helped make people's lives just a little bit easier.

In the Convention Center, an Iraqi Assistance Center was located on the first floor of the building, just below the Media Office, or the Coalition Press and Information Center as it came to be called. Iraqis would line up for hours at the Iraqi Assistance Center, looking for help in obtaining emergency medical supplies, getting back into a home that some Iraqi government agency had forced them out of, and sorting out property.

The Center was run by staff members of the coalition. An American doctor would be sitting next to a Lithuanian typist, who in turn was sitting next to a Polish interpreter and so on. The 41 countries that comprised the US-led coalition were there every day making life different for the Iraqis. The American component, by far the largest, of course, consisted mostly of US military personnel. At the Iraqi Assistance Center the Americans on duty faced all kinds of demanding situations. Did Ahmed's niece need surgery in a hospital that didn't have the facilities in Iraq? No problem, they'd get her to a medical facility in Jordan, or perhaps in Kuwait. Had someone's property been illegally taken over during the chaos of the liberation of Iraq? No problem. The plaintiff needed to produce the land deed, a translation that confirmed the story, and a coalition team would be on its way to the location to ensure that the property was returned to its rightful owners.

The Americans at the Center were tireless, patient, good-natured, often humorous, and somehow always willing to try to help. We were all touched, watching them diligently at work, and it reminded me very much of my dad's motivation for going to Japan in 1951. He, along with my dear mother, had just wanted to help the defeated and beaten down Japanese in response to the call of General Douglas McArthur for 10,000 young people to help rebuild post-war Japan, just as these angels were doing in

Iraq. Once again, all of us were falling in love with them.

The Iraqi Assistance Center was actually next to the large auditorium where the Coalition Press and Information Center was located and press conferences were held. A new, post-Saddam, post-American invasion Iraqi press was slowly beginning to form. The Americans who ran the press office, CPIC as it was called, did what they could to nurture a free press. In fact, the head of the CPIC press office was an American Jewish woman whose parents had fled Baghdad in the 1950s. A short-haired, tough-looking lady, she could be brusque and stand-offish, but she was marvelously efficient. She had obviously volunteered for the assignment while in the United States, as her family had once been part of the booming Jewish community of Baghdad. The irony of her being in charge was not lost on the Iraqis who continued to express often amazed admiration at what the Americans seemed to be trying to do. She was capable and no-nonsense in her dealings with everyone in the media. The press center itself had a score or so of booths in which there was Internet access. Iraqis could come in and use the computers and also, where possible, obtain assistance and advice from the press center. From other offices inside this huge headquarters building, Americans were working hard to help the Iraqis set up the various components of the newly functioning Iraqi government.

The American eagerness to please all comers, to mediate often silly squabbles, to reach out to everyone, came to be seen by some of my Iraqi friends as a weakness. For one thing, the CPA at the outset seemed to be inundated by self-described Islamic experts.

But I had been aware how secular Iraqis had been under Saddam, one of whose sole virtues had been to insist on a legal system modeled on European, secular legal institutions, and not on *sharia*-based Islamic institutions. Iraq was a secular country—

the Baathists, for all their faults, were passionately non-religious. At the press center a garden-variety of Iraqis often showed up with their own particular take on aspects of government and culture in the country. One day when I was there an Iraqi woman walked in. Though the Saddam regime had been far more accepting than most Arab countries of a prominent role for women in society, it was still a little unusual in post-liberation Iraq for a woman to come in without any accompanying male or even a delegation of females with her. Sensing that an interesting story might be at hand, several of the US reporters stopped what they were doing and gathered around the newcomer. Of course, the point of all this was that, following the fall of the Saddam regime, there were hundreds of Iraqis who were speaking freely for the first time in their lives. "I want you to know," she began, "that Saddam and his sons have abused me endlessly. I have waited all my life to say this. I don't care what anyone does to me. They can kill me if they like—I just need to say this. I have waited for 30 years! I myself am a direct descendant of the Prophet, a Sayyed," she said, using the Arabic term that denotes blood decent. That got everyone's attention. "But I have waited all my life to tell my story. Saddam and his sons abused me so much that I don't care what happens now. I don't care if I die tomorrow, but I want to tell the truth. Please listen to me."

I glanced around the circle of reporters listening to her and it was obvious that she had their attention. "They will tell you," she said, not explaining who "they" was, "that Islam is a religion of peace and harmony, but I will tell you the truth. Even though I am a direct descendant of the Prophet, I tell you that the problem with Islam is in the Koran. It is evil. It destroys everything it touches. It is against women and is the source of our trouble."

Some of the Western reporter took all her words down, but I

could tell they were not comfortable with her message. I looked at some of the Iraqi journalists present, however, and two of them seemed to be watching the woman from a physically more distant location in the room. They were fuming, and they were glaring at the woman. Then they began to try to interrupt her and disrupt what she was saying.

I knew exactly what was happening. The Iraqis would call it "the black mind." In those who have it there is the arrogant swagger, the blazing eyes, the often unkempt manner and the strident views that always seem to defy logic but clearly scream "uneducated." I had sat down once with one typical owner of "the black mind" in the press center itself, and he turned out to be one of the men closely staring at the woman. Abbas Moham-med, 24, he had called himself, seemed to take pride in the fact that he had a "black mind."

"I don't care what anyone thinks of me—I believe what I be-lieve and that is all," he had said defiantly.

"What do you think of freedom?" I had asked.

"Man is not free. He is free only to believe God."

"Well," I had responded, "If your son came to you one day and said `Father, I have to tell you the truth, I do not believe,' what would you do?"

The answer was swift and harsh, and his eyes were glaring. "The Koran teaches that at 8 years old you should teach your son, at 10 years you should beat your son. If he does not believe, I will kill him. I will burn him. He does not deserve life."

"What do you think of women?" I asked.

"They are nothing—they are less than 1/10 of man," he growled. At this point in the conversation my interpreter, a woman, had leapt into the fray.

"I cannot continue with this conversation!" she had all but

shouted. "Have him leave." After reciting another catalogue of his favorite hates – the Americans high on the list, of course—he had left, as arrogant in his departure as when we had begun this conversation. Not entirely sure I had heard him right on the subject of his son, I checked with the translator.

"Did he just say that if his son decided not to believe in Islam he would kill him or burn him?" I asked.

"Yes," she had said, her face flushed with anger. "What you have seen just now is 'the black mind'."

Zainab, the translator, seemed as shaken by the encounter as I had been.

"You see, this is the problem! This is our enemy!" she had said. "It is this 'black mind' that is the cause of all our troubles. It is not the Americans. They have come, they have given of their lives. We see them every day, working so hard with us to make things better. It is the 'black mind' that wants to destroy everything! It is the religious leaders that create this 'black mind.' As you can see they are crazy!"

"Where does this come from?" I had persisted.

Zainab had answered, "Maybe 30 percent of the people have connections with Saddam or with 'the black mind'. It comes from Islam. The vast majority of the people, of course, do not think like this, but the 'black mind' intimidates them so they are afraid to say the truth.

"Do you think the women cover their heads and their bodies in winter coats because they want to? No! They do it because they are intimidated by a religious leader, a neighbor, often by members of their own family who are intimidated by some religious leader or other. These men are out of control and someone has to stop them! We are thankful the Americans are trying!

"Many people ostensibly go to the Holy Cities of Karbala and

Najaf to pray. Do you know what the reality is? There are hundreds of women who take two weeks off supposedly to visit the Holy Cities but in fact they go there and make their living as prostitutes. They charge 5,000 dinar, about three dollars each time. This is the reality.

"Do you know what happens in Ramadan, the month of fasting?" She was really gathering steam by now. "They gain weight during the month of fasting. They do not eat during the day because they are intimidated. Then they watch the clock and as soon as it is sundown they begin to eat and drink and party.

"Do you think people pray? They complain at the early morning blaring sounds of the 'call to prayer' from the mosques when they are sleeping! Go to the mosque, other than Friday when many are intimidated into going. Nobody prays! They do not actually believe! It is all a total lie!"

I was shocked listening to this tirade, as I could see many of the Western reporters were. Trying to get something "politically correct" out of the conversation, I gently suggested, "But it is not Islam that is the reason, is it?"

"Yes, it is," she replied. "It is the religious teachers that cause the `black mind,` the mind in which everything is backwards— It is good to kill, women are no good, beat your child . . .this is all crazy! How can any religious person teach this and then say if you don't do as they say they will kill you! What is this?!

"You see," she continued, "it is the religious teachers that are the enemies of Iraq. They block progress for one simple reason— they depend on the `black mind` to stay in power—they create it by keeping people uneducated and under their control. When progress comes, people have freedom and are able to experience and understand truth, then they will realize the problem is the religious leaders and the power of the `black mind` will be gone. This is why they (the religious teachers) are so desperate to see the Americans and the forces of freedom defeated. Because they are desperate to keep the people from becoming educated because they will see the truth."The woman noticed the Iraqis who had been glaring at her drawing closer to her and she sensed that she might be running out of time to tell her tale. She was clearly nervous and she ended her talk by telling the reporters around her to pay attention to what she was saying. "It is all the fault of the Koran," she said, "and political Islam."

Immediately after she had finished speaking, and before she had even left, the two Iraqis who had glared at her as she spoke went up to the supervisor's desk in the press room and complained that the media was slandering Islam. Since they recognized me because I had been associating with and occasionally standing up for the Assyrians, they pointed at me and demanded of the director of the press center that I be removed from the room since I was "offending Islam." I had seen these same Iraqis hanging around the press center before, and was familiar with their intimidating habits. I explained all this to the press center director, the Jewish woman, who was in any case familiar with my work both as a reporter and as a friend of the Assyrians. She told them that they had no grounds for ordering anyone out of the press center purely on the basis of their political or religious views. As they walked back from the director's table one of them passed me and muttered, "Be careful on your way back home." My first official threat in Iraq.

I shot out of my chair and grabbed him by the neck, and as other reporters watched in amazement, I frog-marched him back to the director's desk. "I have just been threatened by this man because of my views on what was being said within this press center," I explained. "This is inexcusable behavior in a press center being run by the Americans. I insist that this thug and his accomplice be expelled from the room." Now the shoe was on the other foot and if looks could kill, I would have been a dead man on the spot. But I felt it was good for the Iraqi journalists in the room to see that threatening and intimidating behavior by people posing as journalists—even if they really were journalists—was totally unacceptable. I suspected it was quite possible that they had gotten their press credentials from the Coalition Press and Information Center without anyone paying close attention to who they really were. Perhaps they were even reporting to Al Qaeda. But even though they had for the time being been expelled from the press center, I knew that I needed to watch my back.

I began to learn that the only way to stand up against politicized Islam—the ideological system embodied by Shariah Law—was to be strong. Standing up to these thugs got me the support and respect from the Iraq journalists who were being bullied by them every day. They derived great satisfaction that someone from the reporting community had stood up to them. That respect and love continues to this day. As far as I know, I am the only non-Iraqi who holds an Iraqi press card. It was a direct result of my standing up to the religious thugs. I can't tell you the name of the Iraqi who made this possible, but it was someone who witnessed what had gone on that day at the press center and years later was in charge of the Iraqi press center.

Just a few days later, after a press conference, I noticed a close huddle of Iraqis in the same press room having an intense discussion. They were both men and women, and the men were wearing beards and the women *hijabs*, the traditional head-covering for religiously conservative Muslim women. It is true that today even in the United States a *hijab* on a Muslim woman is not all that uncommon. Americans like to consider themselves religiously tolerant. Most do not make any kind of fuss over a *hija*b, even if they associate the wearing of it with a form of radical Islam. In Iraq, however, very few women wore a *hijab* because it is such an overt sign of intensely Islamic, indeed even Islamist, sympathies. Men, unless they are very specifically followers of a conservative Islamic leadership, also did not wear beards.

That being the case, the presence of beards and *hijabs* in a close knot of people in the press center was certainly odd. Until relatively recently, wearing a *hijab* or covering yourself were looked on with disdain as something done by the uneducated country people. A look at Egyptian movies up until the late 70s show this in great detail, where the heroes of the movies are always dressed modern and the villains and underclass are always those that cover their heads or are bearded. The view that covering your head and body for a woman, and wearing a beard—the longer the better—for a man, are historically Islamic, is simply not true. It is all a recent phenomenon that has been used politically to force people to conform. Just a few short years ago, in fact, covering one's head and growing a beard were symbols to be ashamed of.

Fred was with me and I asked him to eavesdrop subtly on their conversation and tell me what the buzz of discussion was all about. His answer floored me. "They are organizing a Ministry of Islamic Affairs," he said, almost matter-of-factly. "They are waiting for the Americans to leave so that they can set it up." When I reported this again to the authorities in the press room, these so-called "journalists" were ordered to leave.

Amidst all this the naïve innocence of the Americans in trying to bring order into Iraq, their sheer goodness was touching all Iraqis. One told me, "We know why they are good. It is because they are Christians. We all know the Assyrian Christians and we know that they can be trusted."

Since I had grown up in a country, Japan, in which Christians numbered about 6 percent, I knew that Christian can have an influence in society disproportionate to their numbers. Many of the Japanese prime ministers have been Christian. In fact, Prime Minister Hatoyama's mother has been a supporter of our work for many years. I have known another Christian prime minister, aso, for many years as well. A few years earlier when I had met the emperor and empress of Japan at a meeting, we spoke of the importance of prayer. With tears in her eyes the empress explained how important prayer was for both of them, and we prayed together that God would bless them as well as their country. A few years later I wrote a book with one of Japan's leading Buddhists in which he said, "We need the Christians to be stronger and more influential. It is only they who hold the moral compass for our country." Once again, I was seeing how post-war Iraq resembled post-war Japan.

In 2002, when I had first visited Iraq during the time of Saddam, I recall sitting down with an Iraqi foreign ministry official. I wanted to know how many Assyrians he thought there were in Iraq at the time. He said that the government view was that Assyrians constituted 2.5 million, 10 percent of the Iraqi population. In fact, both during Saddam's era and afterwards I always found Iraqis of whatever political viewpoint—with the obvious exception of radical Islamist political parties, deeply respectful to the Assyrians. Iraqi government ministers, as they came to press conferences at the Convention Center often used to repeat the mantra—a true mantra—that the Assyrian Christians had been the original inhabitants of the country before the Arabs came. It was their country, and whatever they needed would be provided for.

Specifically, it was a chance meeting in New York at the Waldorf Astoria Hotel during the annual United Nations gathering with Iraqi foreign minister Hoshar Zebari in 2007 that got the ball rolling. Waiting in the lobby to meet somebody, I called out to the foreign minister as he walked by.

"Mr. Zebari," I said, "Please help the Assyrians, they really need your help." He paused and told his aids to wait for a minute. This was his response.

"I have a piece of advice for you," he began. "Forget about all your small demands. The most important thing is to get your land. As you know, I am Kurdish, and we have our own area called Kurdistan. The Assyrians are the original people of Iraq. You of all people are entitled to a province of your own. It is stated it in the constitution. Once you have your own land, all of the other problems are solved. Concentrate on this," he said.

"What do we need to do?" I asked.

"You need to make a formal request," he replied. "Why don't you work on a document and bring it back to me tomorrow, and I will take a look at it."

Over the next few hours, we reached out to the Assyrian community all over the world and the next day put forward a formal request for an Assyrian province. Foreign Minister Zebari received it and we received a signed receipt from his staff. A few months later, in a separate meeting with the Iraqi Prime Minister Maliki, he said, "The Assyrians are our best citizens. They are the original people of our country. They are the most patriotic, and of all people, they have the right to be in Iraq."

When I brought up the idea of an Assyrian province that the foreign minister has proposed earlier, Prime Minister Maliki was more than supportive. "That is a wonderful idea. In fact, to help the Assyrians who have already left the country come back, I will do whatever they need to be able to return. I have an interesting proposal. All of the Iraqis receive a monthly stipend for their share of the oil fund. Those that have lived outside the country, many have not received anything from that fund for years. All of those funds are in the account at the ministry of trade, so if you can find the names and the ID numbers of the Assyrians living overseas, we can provide them their share of the oil funds." In many cases, this amounted to thousands of dollars for those that had lived outside the country for many years. "Furthermore," he added, "I propose we, in addition to providing them with their share of the oil funds, provide them with any costs they need to return and to restart their lives and occupations from before, and help to compensate people who are residing in their previous homes." Following up later with his office, and the reality of a dysfunctional parliament who would have to formally approve a province, the prime minister proposed that as he had signed a presidential decree to enable the funds to be provided for those living abroad who wish to return, he would also sign a decree establishing an "Assyrian security zone" which could be done immediately, and over time be ratified officially by the Iraqi parliament. All the Assyrians needed to do was to come up with a general idea of an area to be included in that zone, and begin the process. In closing, he said, "Come back to Iraq. Come and see me and we will give you a desk. Let's work to get all of the Assyrians back home. Whatever we can do, we can do."

As we finished the meeting, I asked, "Prime Minister, would you mind if we had a word or prayer together?"

"Of course," he answered, as he ordered his guards to bow their heads. We prayed together for his protection and health, and for the future of Iraq.

Next, we brought the proposal to Iraqi President Jalal Talibani. Talibani, who was Kurdish, was a dear friend of my mentor, Senator

John Nimrod. He was more than enthusiastic to do anything that would help the Assyrians. His son I knew from Washington was the official representative for the Kurdish regional government in the United States. Talibani's reaction to the idea of an Assyrian province was even more enthusiastic. "This is a great idea," he exclaimed. "Let's do anything we can to get this accomplished." After the meeting, I asked the president if he would mind if we had a word of prayer as well. Jalal Talibani is a big man, and he grabbed my hand, put it on his chest, and said, "I just had surgery on my heart. You must pray right here." We had a time of prayer there for his health and also for the future of Iraq. The next step of the process was a meeting held in December of 2010 in Irbil in northern Iraq, where the main Assyrian political parties gathered together and signed a formal request for an Assyrian province to be delivered to the prime minister's office. To date, as far as we know, the signed document has not reached the office of the prime minister.

In Washington, on various occasions when we had had meetings with US government officials about developments in Iraq, several times we had sensed a real hostility from American officials when we brought up the subject of Iraqi Christianity. We wondered if some of Washington's bureaucrats were altogether unfriendly towards anybody's Christianity, including that of Iraq. On no occasion was the official Washington indifference to the fate of the Assyrians in Iraq more apparent than when Ambassador Paul Bremer, still at the time the American head of the CPA, returned to Washington, DC, in October 2003 for hearings of the Senate Foreign Relations Committee and other Congressional bodies. We had come back from Baghdad to be present at the hearings. We really needed to put in a word for Iraq's Assyrians. In the brief moment before the hearings were gaveled officially open, I asked a question of Ambassador Bremer. "We Assyrians have a very simple question," I began. "Article Seven of the Iraqi constitution states, 'Islam is the religion of the state.' We are very concerned that the current constitution being put together under your direction will be a normal, secular constitution and that there will be local autonomy so our people and others can live freely in the new Iraq the same as we have here in the United States."

I was shocked at his response. "That is something for the Iraqi people and the Governing Council to decide," he said.

I responded that the Iraqi people had been brutalized under Saddam's dictatorship and hardly were in a position to make sound judgments on issues of freedom of conscience.

"Like I said," he retorted, "that is something for the Iraqis to decide."

Seeing Senator Brownback, whom we had met with several times and knew to be a strong supporter of Assyrian Christians, I told him the situation that was developing with Bremer's seeming refusal to support a secular constitution.

"I will have a chance to ask some questions, so why don't you give me some questions to ask Ambassador Bremer?" he said with a smile. I quickly wrote up a series of questions and as the hearing began, I passed them in the form of a note to Senator Brownback once the hearings began to ask a follow-up question to Bremer. When his turn came, reading from my note, Senator Brownback asked the question of the hour— "Ambassador Bremer," he began. "Why are you putting together a constitution for Iraq, in which Article Seven states that Islam is the official religion of the state? It is my understanding that the Iraqi people are very committed to secular government. Why would we be supporting an Islamic government?" In a shocking comment,

Bremer responded by saying, "The Iraqis are Muslims. They should have a Muslim constitution. The British are Christian and they have a Christian constitution. So why shouldn't the Iraqis?" As he spoke, I furiously wrote a note, grabbed one of the senate staff, and asked him to take it immediately to Senator Brownback. Smiling as he got the note, Senator Brownback proceeded to bring the Senate Chamber to laughter. "Ambassador Bremer," he read. "Are you aware that the British don't have a constitution? Are you sure you are the best person to write a constitution for Iraq?" The hearing room erupted in laughter.

It was in fact this failure that in spite of the agreement of the parties drafting the constitution that there be no mention of religion or ideology that caused the current situation where in spite of the clear wishes of the Iraqi people, an Islamist government has taken hold.

There were numerous other incidents during my time in Iraq over the years 2003-2009 when it became clear that the UN and other officials had somehow decided that it needed to show favor, not to Iraqi Christian minorities or the principle of separation of church and state, but to Iraqis who were ardent Muslims. The UN, even before it was blown up by a bomb planted by the insurgent Zarqawi, made it clear that it had no compassion whatsoever for Iraq's indigenous, pre-Arab inhabitants who were Christian. Shortly before it was bombed in 2003, Fred and I and some of the other Assyrians set up a meeting at the newly opened UN headquarters in Iraq. We were ushered in to meet with the head of the human rights office, who appeared to be European. We introduced ourselves as Assyrians and a part of the Assyrian Christiam community and wanted to discuss with him some of the issues our people were facing. Before we had a chance to get into the details, he suddenly stood up, and without blinking an eye said, "This is a Muslim people. Tell your people the best thing they can do is to simply leave." Shocked, we responded, "But, sir, the Assyrians are the original people of Iraq. This is their—our—country." He gestured to the door and said simply, "You can leave." That was one of the clearest indications of the deep-seated bias towards Christians that runs throughout the United Nations, and was much of the source of the cancer that affected post-liberation Iraq. We will never know, but it was only a few short days afterwards that that section of the United Nations building blew up. When they got the news, the Assyrians simply said, "They should learn not to mess with us and our God."

The UN, which is host to 57 nations belonging to the Organization of the Islamic Conference, might be anticipated to have a negative attitude towards Christian minorities living in Muslim states. But what really shocked me was the extent to which a desire to please the Muslims, at the expense of the Christians of Iraq, had penetrated officialdom with the US administration in Iraq. Receiving information that there was a new chaplain in Mosul in northern Iraq, we immediately contacted him to get help for some specific needs that the Assyrians were having. The response was one we will never forget. "My mandate is to help the majority. I do not have a mandate to interact with the minority," he said. In other words, he seemed to be saying his job as a chaplain and as a Christian was to help the Muslim community in his area, but he didn't have time to help his fellow Christians. The response from the Iraqis was heartening. "The Muslims have all kinds of countries helping us. The Americans are Christians. They should be helping the Christians, the ones who need help the most," they said. This was the Iraqi view that in fact both the UN and much of the outside assistance was directed towards Muslims so the Christians were being shortchanged. We continued to press the Christian chaplain, but amazingly, he never waivered. All that we were able to get was a short meeting with some of the Assyrian representatives in the region. It was a telling message that was to have greater ramifications as the dream of the Iraqi people for a secular, modern state was slowly being usurped by a backward-looking Islamic state that the Americans seemed to be encouraging over the objections of the Iraqis.

That this almost toadying approach to political Islam on the part of American officials was not only wrong but not appreciated by many Iraqis of Muslim background became plain to me when I spoke with several Iraqi government officials. After Iraq's first post-liberation elections, a former Iraqi government official of Assyrian background said to me, "It is shameful that the Assyrian Christians who are the original people of the country and should have at least 25 seats in the Parliament have only one seat. Is this democracy? The international community has an obligation to demand that there be proper representation for the original people of the country and to support this."

Another Assyrian friend said to me about American officials administering Iraq, "They don't care about us. We made a big mistake. We thought that they would help us, support us and care for us. We were wrong. The Muslims have many who support them from throughout the Muslim world. It is very strange that the Americans and the EU do not help the Christians. They are the ones that need it the most."

Of course, an Iraqi Assyrian, perhaps embittered by the US government indifference to the Assyrian minority, might have been expected to make a comment like this. What surprised me, however, was the attitude towards the Assyrians of Iraq's Prime Minister Nouri Al-Maliki, whom I spoke with in April 2006. In a wide-ranging conversation, in which he emphasized that he had no timetable for the ultimate withdrawal of the forces of the American-led coalition, Maliki went out of his way to reach out to Iraq's Assyrian Christians. "I have a bias towards the Assyrian Christians," he said. "They are the indigenous people of our country and are our most nationalist and good people. We want them to be inside the country and active and able to retake their rights. We will do all we can to help them. At the same time, if they feel they need an area, a province of their own, I support this fully." The Assyrians had already put in a request for their own province, the only solution, they felt, to the need for security for the country's Christians. Currently, the proposal is that the swath of territory to be made available to the Christians adjoins the autonomous area of Kurdistan. In the same interview, Maliki said that the large number of Assyrian Christians who had fled Iraq after the insurgency got under way were not "refugees" but "displaced." He said that the Iraqi government was doing all it could, including spending substantial portions of its oil revenue, to persuade them to return. The Assyrian Christians have made a formal request for a province in their homeland—a security zone—which many see as the only way to persuade the many outside the country to come home.

I had an opportunity to meet with Iraq's president Jalal Talibani two-and-a -half years later when he was in New York attending the opening of the UN General Assembly in October 2008. One of the disturbing domestic political developments in Iraq since the interview in 2006 with Al-Maliki had been a bill passed by the Iraqi parliament abolishing Article 50 of the Iraqi Provincial Election Law. Article 50 had set aside a designated number of parliamentary seats corresponding to the percentage of Iraq's population occupied by any minority. In Iraq's case, the Assyrian Christians, at the time of the liberation from Saddam, had constituted 10 percent of the population, and the US ought to have held at least ten seats in parliament, as opposed to the two seats out of a total number of 275 that they currently hold. Most Assyrians saw Article 50 as a way of restricting Iraq's ominous drift in the direction of an Islamic-type government. Talibani, a Kurd by nationality, vigorously agreed. "The law just recently passed," he said, "is not consistent with the constitution nor with what we feel is needed for Iraq. We need to do all we can to help those who are currently displaced to return home. As president I have the right to amend what parliament passes and I can assure you that we will be amending the change in the law immediately. We need to protect our minorities and this change sends exactly the wrong message. We are doing all we can to help those displaced to return and recently have put together a plan to provide 10 million dinars (approximately $8,500) to all who return as well as help in building a home and starting a business for all." He added, "We need to get a message to the Assyrians and others that now is the time to come home. Whatever they need we will do for them."

Currently efforts are underway to find the name, ID number and hometown of each refugee so that this payment can be provided to them. In further negotiations with the Minister of Migration and his wonderful staff, the Iraqi government has promised to pay the transportation costs for all refugees to come home, payment to restore their homes, payment to squatters who may be in their homes, and payment to restart their previous small businesses and more. People forget that in fact Iraq sits on the second largest oil reserves in the world and still keeps much of the socialist system which provides from the oil fund for monthly payments to all citizens.

On the US side, in addition to Sam Brownback, we were surprised at those who supported the Assyrian cause. Naturally we thought John McCain would be a logical supporter. My father had been a friend of Senator McCain's father for many years. As the head of the Pacific forces, he was well known as a very godly man who would spend an hour or more in prayer every day. Speaking with my father one day he said, "Brother Joseph, would you pray for my son. He is away from the Lord and messing with women and crashing airplanes." Little did I know that many years later we would be dealing with his son. Senator McCain was on the Armed Services Committee and Foreign Affairs Committee, so we met regularly with him about the Assyrian Christians.

Next we approached another member of the Armed Services Committee to try and get some help for the Assyrians. Having grown up in a very conservative family, we knew the Clintons. They were liberal and we expected no help or support. Further, Hillary Clinton came off as mean and cold. However, our approach to Hillary brought quite a different response. "Sit down and please tell me about the situation," she said. Shocked, I immediately told the story of how the Assyrians were suffering and the ways they could be helped. Then she said the magical words that we knew made the difference: "Help these people out," she told one of her aides, and we knew this was going somewhere. Hillary Clinton, in dramatic contrast to her often perceived public persona, could not have been nicer as she proceeded to listen to our situation, and to date has helped in every way she can. In a follow up meeting in Baghdad, she continued to express her support for the Assyrian Christians and her dedication to doing anything needed to help them. In a humorous aside, shortly after I was in the bathroom of the Waldorf Astoria Hotel in New York. A good place to meet important people if you need to, the bathroom should be more aptly referred to as a living room, complete with sofas and tables. While there, I noticed in passing a couple of mean-looking security guys standing at the entrance. Turning to my right, I was shocked to realize I was standing next to former president Bill Clinton. Thinking that I probably wouldn't have a chance like this again, I quickly turned to him and said, "President Clinton, sorry to bother you, but I'm working with Assyrian Christians of Iraq. Can I talk to you for a second?"

He looked at me with a big smile and said, laughing "You're good! You picked the only place in the world where I come that the security guys don't follow me." He then added, "Could you wait till I finish?" There sitting in the bathroom of the Waldorf Astoria, with the security guys constantly peeking in to make sure everything was okay, I was able to explain the situation of the Assyrian Christians of Iraq. He offered his help and the help of his office with anything that we needed.

Next, was the Chairman of the Foreign Relations Committee. As a Democrat, we didn't expect Senator Joe Biden to be helpful, but as Chairman of the Committee, it was important to talk to him. Approaching him after a committee meeting, I asked if he would have a moment to talk with us about the Assyrian Christians of Iraq. Senator Biden stopped and enthusiastically said, "Whatever we can do to help. You know my proposal that they call the "Biden Plan." It envisions allowing Iraq to become a federation of different ethnicities—the Shia, the Sunni, the Kurds, and finally the Assyrians. Come to me anytime. I am on your side. Update me on any new developments and get the details to my staff here." Every time we were in Washington, one of the first orders of business was to check out a hearing of the foreign relations committee and update Senator Biden on the latest situation for the Assyrian Christians. After becoming vice president, of course, it has been much more difficult to meet, but we were able to meet him, in of all places, Japan, where he had come to offer his support to those devastated by the terrible earthquake and tsunami. In typical Biden fashion, he went from person to person, shook their hands, asked them how they were, and promised to do all he could to do help. Seeing me in the crowd of people, he smiled widely. "Oh no, you're here too! Don't worry, we are doing all we can to help the Assyrian Christians," he said.

Just to indicate how favorable many people in Iraq are to Christianity, it is worth noting how, at Christmas in Baghdad in 2008, the Iraqi government paid for a huge Christmas commemoration in downtown Baghdad. The decoration was a five-story high painting of Jesus. Explaining the Iraqi government attitude towards Christmas, spokesman Abdul Karim Khalaf said, "On behalf of the Iraqi government, all Iraqis are Christians today." Unfortunately, not all Iraqis felt that way. Ironically, when I was wandering around Washington, DC, in December 2009, I couldn't find any notice, sign, or indication that the approaching holiday was connected with the birth of Jesus.

CHAPTER NINE

THE ORIGINAL PEOPLE OF IRAQ

THE **MOHAMMEDAN THREAT** to the Assyrians actually started during World War I, when almost two-thirds of the Assyrian population of Iraq was subjected to murder and ethnic cleansing by a combined attacking force of Turks and Kurds.
My grandparents, Samuel and Marla Joseph, were among those
who succeeded in fleeing the massacre, having been told that
they would have to kiss the Koran as a sign of their adherence to
Islam or suffer death. Faced with genocide in our home village
of Mahoudi in northern Iraq, my grandparents escaped just in
time, walking across the border into Iran on their way to Russia
where they thought they would be protected as fellow Christians. Unfortunately, arriving in Russia, it was the beginning of
the Bolshevik revolution, in which Russia would turn from an
orthodox Christian nation into an athiest, communist country
with no place to shelter prosecuted Christians. Unable to find
refuge in Russia, they proceeded on to London where they re-

ceived word that many of the Assyrians were gathering in Chicago, which was providing refuge as well as jobs in the auto and other industries in the area. My grandfather worked for many years in the hotel industry in Chicago. My grandmother had wanted to become a missionary, following in the grand tradition of the Assyrians having been the ones who first brought Christianity to Europe and Asia, but her dream had been cut short by the Assyrian genocide. One of the most lasting memories of my grandmother is the worn area in front of her bed where she would kneel every day to pray for us. One of my most favorite foods is boiled chicken and rice that she used to make, as well as "dolma" which is a dish made with onions, tomatoes, and green peppers, in olive oils, hollowed out, and filled with rice and meat.

The situation of the Assyrian Christians under Saddam Hussein was a mixed picture. On the one hand, Saddam was a fervent secularist who didn't mind having Assyrian Christians in his own cabinet. One of the more prominent such figures was Tariq Aziz, Iraq's foreign minister at the time of Iraq's invasion of Kuwait and the First Gulf War in 1991. On the other hand, Saddam's campaign against the Kurds was combined with an ethnic cleansing program by his government to transform the demography of northern Iraq. Saddam's gas attack upon fellow-Iraqis, the infamous Halabja gas assault of March 1988, caused death and destruction among nearby Assyrian Christians too. But both foreigners and Assyrians were shocked in 2004 when hitherto secret Saddam regime documents emerged confirming a thorough and relentless uprooting of Assyrians in the north of Iraq during the 1960's and 1970's. I personally had a chance to peruse a 104-page document of the Saddam era entitled, "The Settlements and Villages of the Christian Assyrians in the Region of Kurdistan Iraq" and chillingly subtitled, "The Contribution of the International Non-Governmental Organizations to the Islamization of Assyrian Villages." The report, which had been designated "for internal use only" (in other words, it was a secret Saddam document), listed 290 villages in northern Iraq which had been forcibly depopulated of their Assyrian inhabitants and renamed according to Muslim requirements.

The ethnic cleansing had consequences clearly seen in Baghdad, to which many of the Assyrian families had moved after being uprooted. They graphically described some of the attacks which had led to their departure from the north. My Assyrian friend whom I called Braveheart, in his later thirties and a seasoned observer of events in Iraq said, "They forcibly came into our villages and ordered our people out under penalty of death. Each time we were replaced in our own villages by Muslims who had come from other parts of the country. It was a careful and organized plan to get all Christians out of northern Iraq, particularly in an area where we have the historical right to be there." My Assyrian friend, of course, had been jailed by Saddam Hussein for his activities on behalf of the Assyrians.

Any follow-through on these ethnic cleansing plans was obviously made impossible by the American liberation of Iraq from Saddam's regime in April 2003. But almost from the moment of Saddam's ouster, Muslim groups, both Sunni and Shiite, did their best to take advantage of the new political environment to pressure Christians in the country to conform to a much more Islamist way of life. In March 2004, I drove down to Samawa, a city far in the Shiite south of the country. In earlier decades, there was a large Christian community in Samawa and even a Jewish synagogue. But now, the senior woman in perhaps the last Christian family in the community, Almas Marcos, her husband Bassam, her mother Muneera, her son Stephan, and two daughters Muneera and Lina, seemed to be the only Christians left in the community. As soon as she stepped out of her front door Almas told me that she had to wear the *abaya,* an all-concealing black cloak that is required of devout Muslim women, for fear that she might be attacked or worse if she didn't conform to Islamist pressures. Though she had never previously worn Islamic dress, Almas explained to me that she now felt that there would be physical danger to her and her family members if she did not conform.

Within months of the arrival of the Americans, these kinds of pressures were being placed on Iraq's Christians all over the country. Some Assyrians tried to warn the American authorities that they would likely soon be under direct attack from Islamists, some of whom, like Abu Musab Al-Zarqawi, had taken advantage of loosely controlled Iraqi borders to penetrate the country. Assyrians were also furious that the CPA had easily consented to an interim government that lacked even a single Iraqi Christian in the seven-member Executive Council and was represented by only one Christian in a 32-member cabinet. That one position was given to Pascale Isho Warda, an Assyrian Christian woman who held the title of Minister of Displacement and Migration. Iraqi wags dubbed this the "Ministry of Emigration." The unsubtle message of this position was that Assyrian Christians should simply leave Iraq and emigrate, like the UN had so rudely told us shortly before their headquarters had blown up. "I am very, very angry," 43-year-old Tarik (he declined to tell me his last name), an Assyrian Christian from Baghdad told me. "We are the original people of Iraq. It is not us who should leave Iraq, it is the Arabs that have abused us for centuries that should. We are angry that they insulted us like this. We are sick and tired of being abused, taken advantage of, and intimidated. We will not take it anymore!"

But the apparently insulting attitude of the interim government to the Assyrians was followed by some much harsher actions against them. In August 2004 four Assyrian Christian churches were suddenly bombed in Iraq, four in Baghdad and one in Mosul. The churches were attacked just as worshippers were leaving after Sunday services. The church bombings came on the heels of a series of bombings of Assyrian-owned Christian businesses and homes. In one particularly gruesome incident, two children, ages 6 and 16, were shot in cold blood inside their home. A few days after the bombings, an Islamist website calling itself the "International Islamic Information Site" issued a statement signed by the "Committee of Planning and Follow Up in Iraq." The statement brazenly stated, "Your striving brethren were able to blow up four cars aimed at the churches in Karrada, Baghdad Jadida (New Baghdad) and Dora while another group of Mujahedeen hit the churches in Mosul. As we announce our responsibility for the bombings we tell you, the people of the Cross, return to your senses and be aware that God's soldiers are ready for you. You have wanted a Crusade and these are its results. God is great and glory be to God and his messenger. He who has warned is excused."

Braveheart told me, "We are receiving reports almost daily of someone in our community being killed, threatened, their business being burned or destroyed."

A particularly brutal case involved a 14-year-old Assyrian Christian boy who was in a store in Baqouba, 30 miles to the northeast of Baghdad, when Islamist insurgents entered it. They began to ask for ID's from everyone. Ayad Tariq's ID, as is common in most Islamic countries, had the term "Christian" on it.

"Are you a Christian?" they asked sneeringly.

Without a moment's hesitation the teenager proudly stood up and replied, "I am a Christian."

Then several of the insurgents grabbed the boy's arms and legs, shouted *Allahu Akbar* ("God is great, God is great"), and with agonizing slowness proceeded to sever his head from his body. His words, "I am a Christian" went throughout Iraq and around the world. Many Assyrian Christians stood up, once again, for their faith during a very difficult time.

The killing of individual, targeted Christians went on in both 2004 and 2005. In Basra, which was administered by British military forces, two Assyrian Christian sisters, Janet Sada, 32, and her sister Shada, 25, were killed on the way to work in the city. Working for a British company as translators it is likely—and was certainly believed at the time—that they were targeted by terrorists. For their safety, they had actually been living in Basra's St. George`s church. But that didn't protect them.

There were further killings in Baghdad and Mosul as well. In fact, by the summer of 2009 Mosul, in past decades a relatively peaceful city in terms of communal relations, and near the site of the Biblical city of Nineveh, had become one of the most dangerous cities for Christians in Iraq.

In Baghdad, the Islamist thugs were sometimes more subtle. One morning in 2003 two well-dressed and well-spoken Iraqis wearing beards showed up at the front door of the Assyrian secretary to the archbishop of Iraq. They rang the bell, and when he came to the door said this: "Good morning, dear sir. We are visiting the neighborhood and letting you and your neighbors know that this area is now part of the Islamic Republic of Iraq. We are encouraging all the neighbors (it was an Assyrian Christian neighborhood) to become Muslim. If you choose to not do so you can either pay the *jizyah* tax (required to be paid by all non-Muslims in Muslim-ruled societies under the category of *dhimmi,* or 'protected'). Or you might want to consider moving." It was no different than the methods used over all time to massacre the Christians, the Jews, and anyone that stood in the way of the Islamic hell that turned the Middle East from the center of civilization and progress into a failed area. Many view the current problems in the Middle East in a much simpler way. Bat Ye'or in her books *The Dhimmi: Jews and Christians under Islam* and *The Decline of Eastern Christianity under Islam: From Jihad to Dhimmitude : Seventh-Twentieth Centuy* traces the actual pattern in the Middle East. In fact, the Arabs were never a factor in the Middle East, being nomadic. They derived their survival from simple produce and in a large measure from banditry in which they stole from the massive Christian and Jewish communities that ran the Middle East. Bat Ye'or describes the reality of Islam as no more than a parasitic tribal community organized by Mohammed.

Most people don't realize that in fact the Middle East was formerly not only not Arab, but not Muslim. The Arabs were simply nomadic tribes who lived in the desert and raided the Christian and Jewish communities that were the cities of the former Middle East. With the rise of Islam, the Arab nomads began to become bolder in raiding the cities and then began to develop the system of *jizyah* that ultimately drove the Christians and Jews out of the Middle East, at which point there was nobody left to tax anymore, which is the real root of the current problems of the Middle East, where the non-Muslims have been driven out along with their economic capacity, which was what sustained the Middle East throughout its history. The concept of *"dhimmi"* began to change. Under Mohammed and his successors, the Arabs began attacking and raiding the Christian and Jewish communities. The Assyrian Christians and their brethren were slaughtered en masse. Those left under the *dhimmi* system became slaves. This concept worked while the Christians and Jews were the vast majority. However, with the Shariah Law and the parasitic nature of the tax on the *dhimi*, the Christians and Jews and other non-Muslims began to leave thus changing the face of the Middle East from the majority of Christians and Jews being overrun by Arabs under the influence of Shariah Law. With the promised percentages of all they could steal, and the promised virgins and pleasure they would receive in heaven, they plunged into the killing sprees that continue to this day.

However, they began to realize that by massacring the Christians and Jews, they were destroying the golden goose from which they stole. As late as the 1950s the Christian and Jewish population had dropped to nearly 20 percent. Following the formation of the State of Israel, and the imposed cruelties of Khomeini, the Christian and Jewish population of the Middle East dropped to under two percent. Political Islam had finally killed the golden goose that had allowed it to live off the *dhimmi*. Having begun on thievery and raids, without the slaves to live off of it was unable to sustain itself.

The current problems in the Middle East are a direct result of the final departure of Christians and Jews whose religion and world view stress hard work and sacrifice. They have little to do with religion or politics, but everything to do with economic failure. As the son of the founder of Hamas says, economic collapse, no jobs, and this wholesale failure of political Islam and its accompanying Shariah Law which in its parasitic nature needs someone to feed of, is destined for ultimate collapse in the exact same way as Communism, simply because political Islam does not make economic sense.

***

I never could understand the stubbornness of the Assyrians—wanting to remain in a place so fraught with danger. The Assyrians, however, are quick to pull out *The Promise*. In Isaiah 19:23-25, it says: "In that day shall there be a highway out of Egypt to Assyria and the Assyrian shall come unto Egypt and the Egyptian into Assyria and the Egyptians shall serve with the Assyrians. In that day shall Israel be the third with Egypt and with Assyria even a blessing in the midst of the land. Whom the Lord of hosts shall bless saying blessed by Egypt my people and Assyrian the work of my hands and Israel mine inheritance."

The Promise is very clear. One day just as the Jews had been promised in scripture the restoration of their land, which happened in 1948, so the Assyrians were promised their own country. Assyrians of all ages hang on to this promise, and this is what in spite of their terrible suffering in the Assyrian Holocaust and subsequent abuse has kept the dream alive.

The Promise goes further, though, than just the promise of a restored nation. It provides a roadmap to future Middle East peace. The future of peace in the Middle East, according to *The Promise* is an alliance in the region of Assyria, Egypt and Israel joined together to protect the area. Being in the core of the Middle East, it is clear to see how this alliance will be the cornerstone of a future period of peace and prosperity in the Middle East as the historic populations return and restore the balance that has been so skewed following the devastating rise of political Islam which has stolen the hope, future and dreams of nearly one billion people yearning to be free.

Egypt with a predominately Arab population, Israel with a predominantly Jewish population, and Assyria with a predominately Christian population are literal as well as figurative symbols. For those who believe the scripture, there will be, of course, a literal Assyria, Israel and Egypt; but further, it is symbolic of the only hope for the future restoration of the original peoples of the Middle East—the Christians, Jews, and Muslims—living together in harmony and respect for each other. This is the promise the Assyrians hold dear and what gives them hope.

Less than six months after the handover of sovereignty by the Americans to the Iraqis, on June 28, 2004, the country held its first nation-wide election. Although the turnout was high, and it was clearly a sign that the Americans had intended to bring democracy to Iraq, the Assyrian Christians were bitterly disappointed by the way it was conducted. Assyrians told me that in the north of the country, out of 33 designated polling locations only nine were open and out of a worldwide population of at least three million Assyrians, only 32,000 votes were counted nationwide for the Assyrian Christian community.

The UN, which was in charge of organizing the elections, had prohibited participation by any Assyrians living overseas, even though many had been forced to leave Iraq because of threats to their lives and property. More problematically, there was absolutely no assignment of voter categories according to either geographic or religious/ethnic constituency. By contrast, the US system of representation at the federal level ensures that the Senate provides a break on legislation passed by the House of Representatives because senators are elected two per state, regardless of the size of the population of the state. But in Iraq, a system of proportional representation had been devised by the UN whereby the 275 seats of the Iraqi Parliament were simply split on a national basis according to total number of votes cast per party. The United Nations held a press conference to announce the proportional election system. As we analyzed it, we realized that in fact, the proportional system was designed to ensure that the Islamic parties would gain the majority in the Iraqi parliament, for the simple reason that the proportional representation system favors large groups. We attended the press conference and publicly challenged the UN representative that in fact the system they had designed was designed specifically to favor the Islamic parties and ensure that Iraq would not become a secular state, against the clear wishes of its people. The Islamic political parties, of course, with heavier funding and large-scale organizing, had been able to mobilize a much larger electoral turnout than the Assyrians, who were far less numerous at the time of the election than the 10 percent they had constituted of the Iraqi population under Saddam.

But the election did more than indicate that the Assyrians were essentially being marginalized as the CPA gave way to the interim government and a new parliamentary structure began to take place. Iraqi Vice President Ghazi al Jawar told me that he had seen intelligence that up to five million ballots favoring the Islamist parties had been preprinted in Iran and shipped across the border along with forged Iraqi IDs and were the cause of a vote that so surprised the Iraqis, because it was so different from what they had expected.

We had already protested to American officers in Baghdad that Iranian TV was running non-stop propaganda broadcasts into Iraqi homes and had heard in response the absurd argument that "international regulations" prohibited the US from interrupting the hateful tirades. As the elected Iraqi government took shape in 2005, however, there were physical indications even in the Iraqi parliament that Iran was beginning to exercise a powerful influence. Delegations were showing up in major Iraqi hotels

and in the parliament itself with women garbed in the Iranian
wrap-around coat, called a *jalbāb*, and more men sporting the
beards that reflect Shiite Muslim religious piety. In the first few
months after Saddam's overthrow, we were having dinner with
Marcus Paulus, the head of my Assyrian Tiari tribe. I was fond
of him and his family because he had all but ordered me to leave
Iraq just before the American-led invasion, insisting that I tell
the outside world the story of what life had been like under
Saddam. We had been watching TV and suddenly a news flash
came on that "the Hakim family" had crossed the border from
Iran to re-enter Iraq. Marcus Paulus, normally a dignified older
man, started screaming at the TV screen. "Those Hakims!" he
shouted. "It was they who tortured and killed us in Iran. He had
reason to know. He had been held for 14 years as a POW in Iran.
Some of Paul's fellow-prisoners had actually died in captivity in
Iran. What infuriated and baffled him was that the two Hakims
brothers, Muhsin Abdul Aziz and Amman, had been readmitted
into Iraq when the CPA was still the governing authority. It was
the decision of Ambassador Paul Bremer to allow Abdul Aziz
Hakim to join the Governing Council that evolved into Iraq's
Interim Government. It was the ultimate betrayal as far as Iraqis
were concerned, to turn over the governance of Iraq to their ultimate enemy, the Iranians.

"How can the Americans allow such evil killers into our country?" Marcus Paulus asked. "I thought they wanted democracy?
How can they do this?"

Abdul Aziz al-Hakim was actually invited back to Washington to meet with President Bush in the White House. I received word that following the meeting he would be holding a
public meeting. With Marcus Paulus heavy on my heart, I attended. Thankfully after the presentation was over, there was a

question and answer period. And I was able to raise my hand and point blank speak to Marcus Paulus, reminding him of the fact that Abdul Aziz al-Hakim was from Iran, and the Assyrian Christians as well as the Iraqis in general were against what was happening. Needless to say, the room turned suddenly quiet, but immediately following the presentation, I was surprised to find a member of the defacto Iranian Embassy in Washington presenting me with his business card and inviting me to one of the upcoming events. Later, however, the American admiration for the Hakim family turned sour when two high-level Iranian military officers and two Iranian diplomats were arrested in the Hakim family compound.

Even aside from the malevolent Hakim family, however, and the daily Iranian TV broadcasts, the Iranian influence on Iraq in the post-Saddam era is hard to ignore. The fact that 60 percent of Iraqi Muslims belong to the Shia branch of Islam makes them susceptible to ideas and practices originating in Iran, where Shia Islam is the official faith. Millions of Iranian Muslims have poured across the border into Iraq since the downfall of Saddam made the Iraqi holy Shia cities of Karbala and Najaf accessible to Iranians. The US and other coalition forces sometimes found themselves facing insurgents with weapons and explosives that have clearly originated in Iran.

More sinister, however, is the possibility that Iran has been interfering directly in Iraqi affairs through manipulation of its finances. When a British computer expert, Peter Moore, was brought in to investigate software problems at Iraq's Ministry of Finance in 2008, he was quickly kidnapped by unknown assailants. Moore was released in January 2010, though four of his British bodyguards were murdered after their capture along with Moore. The British newspaper *The Guardian* asserted that Moore had been held for part of his captivity in Iran itself, a claim that was confirmed by General David Petraeus, recently retired Commander, International Security Assistance Force (ISAF) and Commander, U.S. Forces Afghanistan (USFOR-A). Formerly, he was Commander of Southcom, a US regional military command, and the general commanding all coalition forces in Iraq. Several prominent Iraqi public figures have complained publicly at Iran's desire to influence the political direction of Iraq.

As is often the case the devil is in the details. One Iranian who was familiar with developments in Iran recalls the time of the revolutionary success of Ayatollah Khomeini in 1979. He told me, "What I see in Iraq is just what happened in Iran. The radical Islamists have tried to do what they did in Iran. They want to have one election under whatever situation they can and then they claim legitimacy for the regime they have installed which, like Iran, will permit to run in an election only those people approved of by the regime." A few years earlier, I rode in a taxi in Toronto. The driver was an Iranian, and as we were talking, I mentioned that I had been with the Shah shortly before his death. The driver—I never got his name—said, "I've never told this story before, but I was one of the students who came with Khomeini on his flight from Paris. We were all young, naïve students who believed he was going to change things for the better. He promised free food, free housing, and that everything would be different. As the months began to pass, we began to notice that not only were things not improving, they were getting worse. Instead of the peace and prosperity that we were promised, we were seeing a clamp down on the media, on human rights, and in particular the women. There was no free food, no free housing, and the economy had in fact collapsed. One day, the group of us students who had come back with Khomeini cornered him and confronted him with what was happening 'You promised all these things. Why have none of them happened?' we asked. He said—and I will never forget the look on his face. He looked at us and laughed at us in derision. 'You fool' he said. 'I lied.' It had all been a lie to trick us into supporting him and his Islamic Republic in Iran which even today is a scourge on not only the Middle East, but also the world."

An Iranian-style Islamist regime would be a disaster for Iraq, not only because it would be a gigantic step backwards for all Iranians. To replace a secular, fascist dictatorship with a religious fascist dictatorship is no improvement for anyone. Overwhelmingly, Iraq's Sunni Muslims would reject it if only because they became used, under the Saddam years, to a limited role for religion in politics. Such an eventuality, of course, would also be a disaster for Iraq's Assyrian Christians and a major set-back to American hopes of introducing more pluralism into the Middle East.

The Iranians were making their presence more widely felt in Iraq. The pilgrim business from Iran, where wealthy Iranians would pay huge sums of money to visit Karbala and Najaf and pay even greater amounts of money to be buried there, was creating a bizarre situation at Baghdad airport. There were two lines—one just for Iranians coming and going, and one line for everybody else. As we waited in line to get into the airport, all the Iranians had a special entrance, and the Iraqi people became increasingly upset at being treated like second class citizens in their own country, as the Iranians walked through without having to go through the line. "This is Iraq, This is Iraq!" they chanted, as the Iranians scurried by. It was the first practical sign we saw of the defacto colonization of Iraq by neighboring Iran.

I remained curious about what had happened to Iraq's weap-

ons of mass destruction, whose alleged presence in Iraq had justified the original American decision to go to war. The accusation
that the assertions of the existence of WMD's had been a lie
by the British and US governments was repeatedly countered
by Iraqi officials themselves. But it was only when I discussed
the issue with a US serviceman in a conversation in Baghdad
that I began to get the impression that clear knowledge about
the WMD's in Iraq had been suppressed by the US government
for all kinds of reasons. One morning, I passed close by two US
military officers in the middle of Saddam's parade grounds in his
palace in central Baghdad, by now, of course, the Green Zone. I
decided to ask a bold question of the two men.

"What happened to the WMD's in Iraq?" I said. "How come
you didn't find them?"

Their faces became flushed with anger. "We can't talk about it,"
they said, suggesting that I had indeed asked a pertinent question. I pressed ahead with more questions, but they wouldn't answer. Just then, one of the officers moved away to check supplies
in a nearby area. For a few short minutes I was with the younger
of the two officers. He was fidgety, but seemed to be desperately
eager to convey something to me.

Just as had happened when I wanted to know about the US
military's failure to control Iraq's borders after liberation, I found
myself in a strange world where I could ask questions, and the
soldier for his part could reply only by asking his own questions. It was quite bizarre. He looked at me with an intelligent
expression on his face. "What would you do," he asked, "if you
discovered something terrible and finally found that it actually
belonged originally to you?" I was really puzzled.

He repeated his question, but phrasing it in a slightly different
way. "What would you do if you were trying to find something

and it turned out to be your own stuff?" Suddenly I realized what he seemed to be saying.

"So you mean you found it all and much of it was our own? Were the WMD's that were found made by the US and our allies?"

The sigh of relief from the soldier, the quick "zip" motion on his lips, the "I didn't say anything" and the big smile, made it clear. As far as I could tell from this strange dialogue, WMD's had been found, and what had been found were items that we and our allies had supplied to Iraq when it was fighting the war with Iran.

I could see that this might well have been true, but I was still at a loss why the discovery had not been publicized.

Iraqis themselves were much less reticent than the Americans. Foreign Minister Zebari in a press conference in 2004 was quite specific in saying that the WMD's had been shipped out to Syria before the war began or concealed at different locations inside Iraqi territory. This claim was repeated, independently, in the book *Saddam's Secrets: How an Iraqi General Defied and Survived Saddam Hussein* by George Sada (Integrity Publishers, 2006). Sada was a general in the Iraqi air force who, among other things, claims that he argued Saddam out of attacking Israel with aircraft-borne chemical and biological weapons during the Gulf War in 1991. Sada, to whom I am distantly related, is a devout Assyrian Christian. He claimed in his book, and later on *The Daily Show* with John Stewart and on *Hannity and Colmes* on Fox News in 2006, that Saddam's WMD's had been airlifted and shipped by truck to Syria a few months before the Anglo-US invasion of Iraq. He said he had been told this by Iraqi pilots whom he knew personally and that there were more than 56 flights in Boeing 747 aircraft and other transport planes converted for cargo usage.

So, an American officer in conversation with me in Iraq, the Iraqi foreign minister at a public press conference, and former Iraqi Air Force General George Sada had all concurred that there had in fact been weapons of mass destruction in Iraq, and in George Sada's case, details the actual removal before the war began. The administration of George W. Bush, however, apparently deemed it riskier to reveal that the US and her allies had supplied Iraq with WMD's than to suppress information altogether about the existence of WMD's and to imply that the search for them had been fruitless. A simple explanation describing the fact that Iraq had earlier been an ally of the West against Iran, and it was at that time that the WMDs had been purchased to protect themselves against Iran. That explanation would have been better than to deny the existence of WMDs which to this day caused the entire liberation of Iraq to be questioned, because its primary reasoning was not correct.

Meanwhile, as we watched the American governance of Iraq change over from the CPA and Ambassador Bremer in 2004 to the Interim Government and Transitional Government, I was convinced that the entire power transition was occurring too quickly.

I had written several articles about why I thought this was the case and warned against a too-rapid handover to full Iraqi control. There had been forty years of Saddam's tyranny, and here were the Americans removing themselves from Iraq's governance fewer than 15 months after freeing Iraqis from his rule. I recalled from my own experience growing up in Japan realizing that 500,000 American troops had come into Japan after that country's surrender and they remained in the country for seven years, and many to this day say that the withdraw from Japan was too sudden, with the change following the outbreak of the Korean war.

Many Japanese have told me that they feel this period was in fact too short and the changes that were imposed on Japan by the Americans didn't go far enough. They believe that many of Japan's current problems today have stemmed from that accelerated changeover.

Many Iraqis, especially the Assyrian Christians and strongly secular Iraqis, kept telling me that Ambassador Paul Bremer gave them the impression that he was eager to wash his hands of the whole business of governing Iraq and that he was always too willing to make concessions to the Islamist component of post-Saddam Iraq. I participated in some of the meetings drafting Iraq's future constitution as an Assyrian delegate. Each of the groups in Iraq—the Shia, the Sunni, the Kurds, and the Assyrians and the Turkoman—and others were part of a bigger committee drafting the constitution. Coming out of one meeting on the constitution, I watched as one of the delegates, a seasoned participant in Iraqi politics even before the era of Saddam Hussein, slumped into his chair. He was weeping.

"I thought the Americans were going to help us become a democracy," he said, almost sobbing. "But they are turning us into an Islamic state. Saddam was bad, but this will be worse. What is wrong with the Americans? We want a democracy, we do not want to become like Iran. All of the groups agreed that there should be no mention of religion or ideology in the constitution. Why are the Americans insisting that we make Islam the official religion of the state?" I was to hear this concern repeated to me countless times in the days that followed in the discussions of Iraq's future constitution.

The constitution of Iraq under Saddam Hussein in a way was a meaningless document. Nobody could challenge Saddam's hold on power without risking his life. But Iraq under Saddam and the ruling Baath Party was a determinedly secular state. Of course, Saddam suppressed the Shia and was brutal towards them. He insisted, however, that Iraq be a secular state and he prescribed an entirely secular-based legal system for the country. There was not a word about *sharia*— Islamic religious law—operating in society while Saddam was in charge of the country.

Nobody, of course, advocated that the new Iraq should emulate any aspect of Saddam's kind of regime. It is a fact, however, that female literacy increased by leaps and bounds during Saddam's regime because, of course, he removed any Islamic restrictions on the education of women. Partly as a result of the educational improvements for women, Iraq's medical system was for a while the envy of the Arab world.

What my disconsolate fellow-delegate at the constitutional discussion had been so depressed about was the decision of the post-Saddam Iraq to introduce one small line into the constitution, a line that contained Article Seven. This stated, quite simply, "Islam is the official religion of the state." I felt that with that one sentence, the battle lines had been drawn. Would Iraq become an Islam country? Or the secular state that Iraqis dreamed of, much like neighboring Dubai?

Many Iraqis told me that they were furious that this article was being inserted into the constitution and that it was being approved, moreover, by the Americans. To many of them it signified that they were going to be ruled, sooner or later, by the mullahs.

One of Iraq's new leaders with whom I had discussions about the Islamic component of the constitution was Ibrahim al-Jaffari, the prime minister of Iraq after the handover of July 2004 moved Iraq from the CPA (Paul Bremer's pro-consulship of Iraq) to the Iraqi Interim Government. I had met him several times in

Baghdad and had an opportunity to sit down with him in May 2004, before the official handover of sovereignty to the Iraqis. I found him to be kind, helpful, and sensitive to the plight of the minorities in Iraq. What I wanted to ascertain from Jaffari was why Iraq was now moving in a political direction that would be a repudiation of the secularism that – in my impression – most Iraqis overwhelmingly favored.

"Mr. Prime Minister," I said, "Why are you advocating Article Seven, which states that Islam is the official religion of the country? The Iraqis do not want this! Why do you keep pushing it?"

"Well, if we did not put Islam as the religion of the state, the Iraqi people would revolt," he replied.

I smiled. "My Jaffari," I replied, "I think you have been outside Iraq for too long (in fact, Jaffari had been in exile from Iraq for 12 years in Iran and then 13 years in the UK) and, forgive me, but I think you have lost touch with your people. They are secular. They do not want an Islamic government."

Suddenly Jaffari lost his temper. "How dare you say such a thing! You know nothing!" he bellowed at me. I thought he was about to punch me in the face. Then one of his aides stepped between us and turned to Jaffari. "Sir," he said "I am afraid he is right."

Given that Jaffari was the head of the Dawa Party, a Shia party dedicated to creating an Islamic state, and was a close confidant of Ali al-Sistani, the leading Shia Ayatollah of Iraq who in fact had been born and raised in Iran, I was not surprised that he reacted to my statement so belligerently. But now he looked at me a little embarrassed, as though his hand had been caught in the cookie jar. "When things settle down," he said, "come and see me again. I will assign a team from the government to go with you all over Iraq and we will do a survey of the Assyrian Christians to find out their needs and to put in place legal provisions to protect them."

While Ambassador Bremer and the CPA were still calling the shots in Iraq, it seemed clear to many Assyrians and other Iraqi minorities that constitutional changes being discussed did not look good for the Assyrians and other minorities like the Yezidis, Shabaks, Manacheans and other non-Muslim minorities.

But the problem was larger than Bremer's ignorance of constitutional history in the Anglo-Saxon world. The fact is that the CPA from the very beginning appeared to have a strong bias against Iraq's Christians and a penchant for supporting Islamists, as we were later to see develop into the so called "Arab Springs." Bremer and his advisors were either unaware of the history— that the Middle East before the arrival of Islam had been Christian and Jewish, and that many millions of Christians still lived in the Middle East today—or just didn't want to recognize it.

It seemed apparent to me and my Assyrian friends that the Americans under Bremer were so afraid of being seen to be in any way favoring Christians that they bent over backwards to give Iraqis the impression that they really wanted to favor Muslim attitudes. Perhaps, because Saddam had been so aggressively secular the Americans may have felt the moral obligation to allow the Muslims of Iraq, both Shia and Sunni, much more slack.

Independently of this fact, I had the unmistakable impression that the coterie of State Department officials surrounding Bremer and giving him advice were themselves somewhat prejudiced against Christians and were decidedly Islamist oriented. Whenever I had met with US officials—other than legislators—in Washington, DC, I was left with the impression that they weren't very comfortable around committed Christians. What seemed to me a very definite mindset seemed to be even more pronounced in Baghdad. Ironically, most Iraqis I met with over many years in and out of the country expressed nothing but sympathy and support for the nation's Christians. They never expressed to me any disgruntlement over the idea that America might want to support the Christians. It was one of the most puzzling phenomena of my experience living and reporting in Iraq: the American officials running the country just didn't seem to want to help Iraq's Christians.

In the Arab Muslim world, however, the stakes for followers of minority faiths are significantly higher than Americans sometimes imagine. I have stark childhood memories of staying in my grandfather's apartment in Chicago and waking up in the middle of the night to hear him screaming. He would wake up screaming, having remembered the terror of the Assyrian genocide. That was the psychological legacy of the Assyrian genocide that had driven my grandparents out of the village of Mahoudi in Northern Iraq. Two-thirds of the total Assyrian population perished in the Assyrian genocide. Sadly, even today in Iraq—as I described in the case of the 14-year-old Assyrian boy—there are times when Muslims enter a Christian village or community and demand that the choice be conversion or death. My own grandparents, as I have previously described, had escaped just hours before the Muslims arrived to act good on their threat. They walked into Iran, then into Russia. From there they traveled to Europe and ultimately the United States where they were processed like tens of millions of other refugees through Ellis Island. Chicago at that time had one of the largest Assyrian communities in the United States, and it was there they made their new home.

Americans, sadly, are surprisingly ignorant of the total absence of freedom of conscience within the Islamic world. It is a freedom that Americans assume is as natural as the air they breathe, but it is almost completely lacking in most Muslim states. In

Saudi Arabia, converting to a religious faith other than Islam is considered "apostasy," a crime under *sharia* law which is punishable by death. In the entirety of Saudi Arabia there is not a single church or temple or recognized place of worship for any religion other than Islam. Not just in Iraq, but in many parts of the Muslim word, if a young person told his or her parents that he – or she – no longer believed in Islam, the response would be, at least verbally, murderous. Even the TV channel Al Jazeera, which broadcasts news in Arabic throughout the Arab world, felt itself obliged to apologize to its audience after permitting an Iraqi exile who was a religious agnostic, Wafa Sultan on February 21, 2006, to attack fiercely Islam during a live broadcast. Of course, Al Jazeera, despite priding itself on being a progressive and cosmopolitan station, gives an inordinate amount of air time to conservative Islamic preachers who do not hold back from attacking non-Islamic religious points of view.

One of the best examples of this was crossing the border into Israel. The first thing one notices is the dramatic difference in the economy. One goes from dusty failure to modern success, much like crossing into West Berlin from East Berlin during the time of Communism. Crossing the border from any of the bordering countries into Israel is like crossing from Africa into Europe. The contrast could not be more stark. After getting into an Israeli taxi with a Palestinian driver on the Israeli side, I began to ask questions for an article I was working on, regarding the much reviled wall that Israel had put up along the border. Fully expecting a tirade of bitterness against the Israeli, I was shocked to have the driver turn around to me, put four fingers to his lips, and blow kisses in the air. With a strong Arabic accent he said, "We thank God every day for the wall!" I asked him why. "My friend," he answered "Before the wall, they used to come in every day and steal, and bomb, and rape, and caused trouble for us. Now with the wall, everything is quiet. We have peace." I was amazed because the view throughout the world was that the Israelis had created a wall of oppression that was reviled by the Palestinians and the world, when in fact, here was someone who was thankful for its construction. As we arrived in Jersusalem, where I had been many times previously, I realized for the first time that all the signs were in Arabic. This was Jerusalem, the capital of Israel, and yet everything was in Arabic! The taxi driver left me off, and I happened to be next to a book shop. There was a newspaper rack, and on the front page of one of the newspapers was a picture of the prime minister with something written below it in Arabic. I asked one of the attendants about it and he told me that it read, "The prime minister is a fool." Then it struck me—the irony, the only country in the Middle East, with the exception now of Iraq, where a newspaper could write, in Arabic, that the prime minister was a fool, was Israel. There were no Jewish communities, or newspapers, or shops or signs in the other Arab countries, and yet here in Jerusalem, the much hated capital which was supposedly abusing the Arabs, the whole area was written in Arabic, and the newspapers were free to criticize the prime minister in Arabic.

In the battle for a secular orientation of the Islamic constitution, one of the symbolic issues was the *hijab*, or Islamic headscarf for women. Throughout the Arab world, even in Egypt, but especially in Iraq, women tended not to wear the *hijab* because they associated it with the subordination of women from which they were trying to escape. I discovered in attending the constitutional discussions on behalf of the Assyrians that the *hijab* was used as a wedge issue to push for many other changes in society favorable to Islam. The argument presented would be that the

hijab was merely a "cultural" issue. But it has become clear by observing the regime in Iran that dress code regulations have in fact
become a means to exerting political control. When Khomeini
came to power in Iran in Frebruary 1979, women were required
to wear not merely the *hijab* but a long and stiflingly heavy top-
coat, the *jilbāb*, as well. Turkey, a Muslim-majority country that
has nevertheless been determinedly secular since its founding by
Mustapha Kemal Attaturk, in 1923, has actually banned wearing of the *hijab* on government-controlled spaces; for example,
on the campuses of Turkish state universities. That law is still in
place today. The reason is not that the Turkish government is
paranoid about Islamic fashion statements, but because it understands the *hijab* as a symbol of the transformation of Turkish
society into a religious entity quite different from the secular society modern Turkey's founder had in mind. The male equivalent
of the *hijab* was the wearing of beards by Islamic men.

The inauguration of the first Iraqi government after the
transfer of sovereignty in June 2004 took place on June 28. The
event, as I have described, took place in the basement of one
of Saddam's palaces, which American troops had worked hard
to transform into a room with fitting dignity for the occasion.
Many Iraqis, however, were paying less attention to how neat the
room looked, but how women would be dressed who appeared
on the stage of government representatives. Would they be wearing the *hijab* or not? At the beginning of the event, a Muslim
imam dressed in white but wearing tennis shoes began with an
opening Muslim prayer. He was droning on and on and I for
one was really dismayed by the Islamic religiosity that seemed to
be overlaying the proceedings. I started coughing in a desperate
attempt to disrupt things. American security personnel came up
to my seat and asked if I needed any assistance. I waved them

away and continued to cough, to the delight of Iraqis present who shared my dismay at the Islamic "creep" into government that they saw happening before their eyes. Prayer in itself at the outset of the meeting would not have been inappropriate. It just ought to have been prayer by representatives of many of Iraq's religious communities, not just of Islam. The tennis-shoe imam finished his long droning prayer then high-tailed it to the back of the room where tables had been laid out with copious helpings of food. Iraqis close to me rolled their eyes at this display of gluttony coming hard on the heels of public piety. Some of them commented, "Typical iman. They are all the same, here just for the food."

It is hard for me to exaggerate the sense of disappointment that many Iraqis in the room seemed to feel about this obvious leaning of the new government towards Islam. One Iraqi at the event said to me, "Why would the Americans want to install an Islamic government? We just got rid of Saddam Hussein, why would we want a dictatorship of the mullahs? What's wrong with the Americans?"

I had no ready answer. I had watched with dismay as the CPA under Ambassador Bremer had bent over backwards to offer favor to the Muslim clerics of Iraq. I can only conclude that Americans think they will be liked if they promote someone else's religion when they are in a position to do so, regardless of the fact that this religion may actually be very offensive in its daily activities to the citizens of that country. We repeated to every American official I could persuade to meet me in Iraq that the Iraqis didn't want an Islamic dictatorship imposed on them after they had just been delivered from Saddam Hussein's Baath Party megalomania. I can't help concluding that part of the American reluctance, at the official level, to insist on a secular constitution for Iraq is derived from the simple fact that they either could not or would not understand that in fact someone could be an Arab and not be a Muslim, and in fact not want a religious government, just like the Americans had pioneered in their constitution. And I can't help feeling that, in the rarified intellectual atmosphere of nearly all of the State Department officialdom surrounding Ambassador Bremer, only Muslims were listened to, not Iraq's Christians, or anybody else's Christians.

I first had an intimation of what political/religious process might be insinuating its way into Iraq quite soon after the American liberation of Baghdad. It was July 2003 and I was in the lobby of the Palestine Hotel. As foreigners and Iraqis in the lobby watched in amazement, a delegation of Iranians trooped in. You could tell instantly that they were Iranians, both from the shabbiness of their clothing in general and because the men, almost all of whom had beards, were not wearing neckties, a political no-no in the Islamic Republic of Iran. They all also seemed to have pasty white faces. The women in the group wore not only *hijabs* but the suffocatingly all-inclusive Iranian-style women's "winter coat," the *jilbab*.

Wandering into the Al Rasheed Hotel in Baghdad and observing a large group of women dressed in very conservative Islamic fashion, I thought at first it was an event associated with the nearby Iranian embassy. I learned to my amazement and dismay that the event had been co-sponsored by the Iraqi government and the UN for International Women's Day. The Iraqi manager at the hotel was as dumbfounded as I was, for Baghdad likes to think of itself as a cosmopolitan city. "This is Baghdad," lamented the manager, pointing despairingly at the women. "Do you see this? They all look like they are from Iran. What is our country coming to?" he wailed.

I found one of the conservatively dressed women and persuaded her to talk. "Why is everyone dressed like this?" I asked.

"Please don't misunderstand," she said apologetically. "We don't dress like this normally. It is too hot and this is not our style, but if we do not, they threaten us," she explained. A friend standing by her side nodded in agreement. Another woman, a member of the election committee, explained that they were told to dress that way and wear a coat, even in summer, if they wanted to be on the committee. I wanted to know who "they" were. "Iran is taking over everything," the election committee woman explained.

Another woman, an Iraqi Assyrian Christian, refused to take part in a business meeting organized for women, because she said she was afraid she would be seen.

"By whom?" I asked. After all, we were inside the Green Zone, supposedly protected by the US military.

"I'm so sorry," she said, "but they will see me and it will be a problem for me." She was obviously genuinely frightened. "They are from Iran," she added, "They are everywhere. If I am seen they will cause trouble for me. They have hurt many."

I repeated the gist of this dialogue with the Iraqi-American who had been coordinating the event.

"I am afraid she may be right," he said, almost in a whisper. "There are Iranians all over the place," he added. "They are everywhere. They have forged IDs stating they are Iraqi."

Another woman who had removed her head-to-foot covering related the story of her "arrest" and a detention which lasted for six hours, apparently by actual Iranians in Baghdad. "They were all Iranian and influenced by Iran," she said. "The only way they let me go was if I promised I would spy for them inside the Green Zone and with my contacts." Understandably, she asked that her name not be used in my account of what had happened.

For the Iraqis, used to Western-style fashion even under Saddam, the appearance of the Iranians made their jaws drop. In the days and weeks ahead they would be forced to endure what some of them told me was "colonization" under Iran. Within months the poor Iraqi women were forced to not only to cover their heads but dress in the hated conservative Islamic garb so common in Iran.

The big lie is that this is how they have always done it. This simply is not the case. As any woman in the region will tell you is, until the rise of Khomeini in Iran and the resurgence of radical political Islam, women never covered their heads. It was a sign of oppression.

Ironically, a study in Jordan came up with an interesting discovery. Ostensibly, the reason for covering the women so no flesh could be seen was to protect them from sex-crazed men. In fact, it had the exact opposite effect. The study, which was reported in the *Jordan Times,* concluded that by covering themselves, the women of the Middle East faced a greater number of sexual assaults. The reason was that since men could not see their form and, in many cases, their face, they would attack women that they normally would not have attacked. Further, another study showed a strong effect on the women's health. Covering their bodies, head, and, in many cases, faces resulted in women not taking care of their bodies, resulting in serious health problems.

***

A statistic quite often thrown around in conventional commentary on television and in the print media is that there are "one billion Muslims" in the world. What almost nobody looks into is how many of those one billion really believe in their faith, or have the slightest respect for their mullahs, whom they refer to as imams. I've had many conversations with Iraqis, and not just with Assyrian Iraqis, who make clear their disdain for the Muslim clergy of their country. A typical reaction that I hear from Iraqis is, "Imam? They are all bad. No, maybe 5 percent are good, but the rest are all bad!" I've actually talked to many people who have said that they have heard this view expressed not only in Iraq but wherever in the Muslim world people are free to talk.

In another incident while waiting in Amman to return to Iraq I was trying to find a place in the city to buy a phone card to add time to my mobile phone. "You need to go to the religious bookstore," I was told. It wasn't immediately apparent to me what the connection between mobile phones and religious bookstores was, but I went anyway. It was across the street from the former main bus station in Abu Dali in downtown Amman.

It certainly was "religious." The store shelves were piled high with Korans of various sizes and designs, and the other books there all seemed to be about Muslim religious topics. There was a musty atmosphere to the place; it was obvious that nobody was buying religious books. Standing at the counter I saw what appeared to be the person in charge at the back of the store. He was on a prayer rug and doing the Islamic prayer.

As I looked on, his cell phone rang. Until that moment he had been busy speaking out the Arab words of his prayer. To my great amazement he effortlessly picked up his cell phone, put it to his ear as he continued to bow up and down, and began a conversation on the telephone, interrupting it to continue his prayer. I was, well, "shocked" is the right word at this incredible, effortless "talent" of praying and talking on the telephone at the same time. He finished, rolled up his prayer rug, folded it away on a shelf and turned towards the front of the store. Finally, he saw me waiting. He began to acknowledge my presence as he walked slowly to the front of the store, but just then looked beyond me outside and started blowing kisses into the air. I turned to see what it was, and saw a girl walking by.

I stepped up to the counter and said "What are you doing? I just watched as you prayed and talked on the telephone at the same time. I would think that at least for a few minutes after your "prayer" you would be good, but the first thing you do after praying is leer at a pretty girl. What is this?"

As I said this, I realized I was watching a piece of the reality of the Islamic world. Of course, there are some genuinely pious Muslims who take their religion and its demands on their personal lives seriously. But even in this "religious" bookstore it was quite clear that multitudes of supposedly serious Muslims live a sort of split existence, publicly declaiming by their profession and sometimes even their clothes a commitment to their faith, but privately being as worldly in their way as anyone else at large.

The salesman grinned at me and said, "You got me!" He admitted quite frankly that he was a hypocrite. But he also revealed inadvertently that much of the public piety in the Arab world is often totally insincere. Anyone who has spent any time in the Muslim world during the month of Ramadan will recognize this. Ramadan is a month of fasting which moves through the year according to the lunar calendar. Fasting during it is one of the "five pillars of Islam," a requirement of behavior for all serious Muslims. The other four are 1) *shahada*, the profession of faith (i.e., saying, "There is no God but God and Mohammed is his prophet) ; 2) prayer five times a day at designated times; 3) the payment of a tithe (in Islam 2 ½ percent of one's earnings in this case, not ten percent as in the Jewish and Christian traditions); and 4) the *haji*, or pilgrimage to Mecca.

Now the form of fasting at Ramadan is obviously not refraining from food or drink for the month, which would be impossible for any human being. But it is refraining from food or drink during the daylight hours. In fact, there are huge meals just before dawn and the beginning of the daytime fast period, and huge meals once the fasting time is over and night has officially begun. In theory, the purpose of Ramadan is to turn your mind away from matters of the stomach to concentrate on God. In practice, more food is consumed and people add more weight to their bodies by eating unnaturally throughout the Islamic world during Ramadan than any other period of the year. People are constantly looking at their watches to see how much longer they have to wait before they can gorge themselves.

As a matter of course in conservative Muslim countries a woman's testimony in court is equal to only half a man's. It was probably in realization of how this repression of women would have harmed Saddam's goals to improve literacy among Iraqis and gain the most productivity from them that Saddam Hussein—again, in no way overlooking his ruthlessness and wickedness—made Iraq far more respectful of women's rights than most of the remainder of the Arab world. Women played a major professional role for decades in Iraqi society. They did not cover their hair and they prided themselves on their educational attainments. By contrast, in the Shiite parts of the Islamic world, including Lebanon and Iran (which is not Arab, of course), the practice of "temporary marriages" by which men can "marry" a woman for a few days or even hours and then "divorce" her has led to a high degree of prostitution which is, of course, "legal." In modern-day Iraq, now that Saddam's restrictions on the Shia have been entirely lifted, such prostitution is very common on the heavily Shia south of the country. The authorities content themselves that these religious contortions are within the legal limits of a politicized Islam, but more than likely it is the huge income from the Iranian pilgrims that bend the law.

Well into the modern era, it was partly because of these restrictions on Muslims that Christians and Jews and other religious minorities played such an important role in the economic lives of Arab societies. One reason was that Islam prohibits the application of interest to loans, the very principle without which lending and capitalist development cannot take place. During my period in Iraq over several years, many Iraqis told me that they had noticed an Islamic "creep" taking place in their society, with an increasing number of women wearing the *hijab*, and even the Iranian-style *jilbab* overcoat. Many of them expressed their disgust to me. Worse, it seemed to be happening with the blessing of the American authorities who had entered Iraq promising democracy and freedom and seemed to have been seduced away from these notions by the politically correct idea of "honoring" Islam. The "honor" was not one that most Iraqis I spoke to wanted to have any part of.

The discrepancy between Muslim claims of moral uprightness and the frankly cynical behavior of so many ordinary Muslims is a topic I had the opportunity of discussing during my time in Amman before my return to Iraq after the fighting was over. I asked to be introduced to an imam who could take the time to meet with me and discuss a number of issues. One day I asked him, "Imam, let me know the real truth. How many people really believe in Islam? What percentage of the people do you think really believe without the force of law obliging them to do so?"

He smiled, thought for a bit, and then said, "Maybe three percent, four percent. Probably less. That is the basic problem with Islam. Because we have forced it on everybody, nobody really believes. Of course, they are described as believers simply because they are born in Muslim countries. But they go through their daily prayer only because if they don't someone will beat them or they will lose their jobs. They are born into a faith that they did not choose and they don't actually believe."

I was amazed. Of course, I had made similar observations myself, but I had never heard a Muslim imam admit this so candidly. (My own impression is that, if free from the external Muslim constraints; i.e., a society where alcohol is prohibited and the morals police are active, Muslims often drink, abuse women, and worse. Islam is not a faith but an abusive political system.) I wondered about the analogy of Islam to Communism; a totalitarian belief-system that no one believes in but yet it is kept going by fear. I couldn't help but think that the reaction of many Muslims might be similar to what one used to hear from people trapped within Communist societies: "This is all a monstrous lie. Please help us escape from it."

That perception of Islam, of course, was not the one entertained by the CPA, the State Department advisors assisting it, or anyone else guiding American policy towards Iraq. The CPA policy seemed to be to favor the Muslims and hence earn brownie points for a United States.

I realized this when I tried to get in touch with American military chaplains in Iraq and find out why there seemed to be such reluctance to help the Assyrians. The vast majority of US military chaplains, however, reflecting the heavy Christian majority of personnel in the US military, are Christian. Yet I was shocked to learn what their apparent orders were, when in Iraq, in regard to the indigenous Iraqi Assyrian Christian community.

As an MK in Japan, I had grown up with American military chaplains. Almost invariably, they were down-to-earth people who liked to help out in very practical ways the families of people on American bases. They would always be willing to help with furniture, supplies and encouragement, not just to service personnel under their charge, but to the local Japanese churches.

I first learned that something was different about Iraq when some Assyrians came to me and said, "We don't understand. The Americans are helping the Muslims, but they are not helping us."

The Assyrians kept telling me that they felt unfairly dealt with in Iraq's new political system. They had only one seat in the Parliament whereas they felt that, in proportion to their numbers in the Iraqi population (about 2.5 million out of 25 million, as I was told by Saddam officials) they should be fielding about 25 members of parliament. They complained to me that they had been shut out of most aid programs, now had about 500,00 of their community in refugee camps in neighboring countries, and had, moreover, been turned away from jobs. They claimed to me that government jobs were routinely going to Muslims only, rather than to a broad range of the Iraqi population, which would certainly include anything up to 10 percent of the Iraqi population.

I arranged for a special meeting for some of my Assyrian friends with one of the chaplains. As it happened, however, a few days before the scheduled meeting I was with some Assyrians in the lobby of the Rasheed Hotel and we found ourselves sitting next to the very chaplain we were scheduled to meet. He and his assistants were in an intensive discussion with the Chairman of the Islamic Party of Iraq. We were, I'm a little embarrassed to say, eavesdropping and heard snatches of conversation about assistance that the US could provide them. Essentially, what was happening was that the business that had formerly been conducted in the Convention Center at the Iraqi Assistance Desk was now being conducted at the Al Rasheed Hotel. There, it turned out, many American officials were locked in discussions with Islamic groups—some from Iraq, some from elsewhere—while the Assyrian Christians were being completely ignored.

"It's a waste of time," said one of the key Assyrian leaders and a former Minister in the Government who I had persuaded to attend the meeting. The Americans only care for the Muslims. They are not going to help us."

I persuaded the Assyrian group, however, to keep the appointment with the senior chaplain. Despite their overall pessimism, they agreed.

The Assyrians certainly gave the chaplain an earful. They told him that they had been shut out of parliament, they had friends and relatives among the 500,000 Assyrians in refugee camps outside the country who were getting no assistance at all from the Americans, they were unable to return to their homes in either Baghdad or other parts of the country from which they had been driven out.

The chaplain, who had been eagerly discussing aid to Iraqi Muslims just a few minutes earlier, grew visibly more irritated with this litany. Finally, when they paused for breath, he said to them, "Why don't you just leave?"

The Assyrians were furious. Knowing, as they did, how he had been reaching out to the Muslims of Iraq, and how the Americans had been singularly uninterested in the Assyrian situation as a whole, it was the last straw. But they didn't explode in front of him. One of them said, "Leave? This is our country! We were here long before the Arabs arrived! How dare you help a Musim and yet tell us to leave!" One of them shrugged at me and got up to leave. I indicated politely to the chaplain that he might have said something more diplomatic to them. But he apparently didn't care.

We drove back to their homes in complete silence. I was acutely embarrassed that an American Christian chaplain, and someone whom I had actually gone to school with, had dismissed fellow-Christians in Iraq as though they really had no right to be in the country at all. The Assyrians, aware that they were supposed to be exercising the Christian virtue of patience, bit their tongues in anger and disappointment.

Finally, one of them said with great bitterness, "They are Americans! They are supposed to be Christians! We expected them at least to help us as fellow-believers. We thought at least that they might be fair, but they apparently want to help only the Muslims of Iraq. The Muslims of Iraq have so many countries sending them help. Why can't the Americans help us? Perhaps they have some secret plan to turn Iraq over to the Muslim political parties."

I realized I had to set about tracking down whoever might be in charge of the various US aid programs for domestic Iraqi projects. It was difficult. There didn't seem to be any one person who was overall in charge of US economic assistance programs for Iraq, at least in Baghdad. I finally located an entity called the "Provincial Reconstruction Teams." American government agencies such as USAID and other aid groups had joined together to form Provincial Reconstruction Teams to identify aid needs in Iraq and handle those needs. When I found someone from this organization willing to meet with me, I recognized that person and nearly all of his staff as Americans I had noticed many times in the Al Rasheed Hotel meeting with various Muslim and political groups.

I made the point that the Assyrians were complaining that no one was helping them and I therefore wanted to know if anything could be done for them. I had barely finished the sentence before the reply came back, "We don't work with any particular religious group."

"Fine, but the Assyrians are telling me that you are dispensing plenty of money to Muslim groups and nothing to the Assyrians."

He didn't say anything directly but gave a half-shrug and then, looking at his watch, he said he had to go. I persisted. "Please, it has taken a lot to arrange a meeting with you like this. Please go over the programs that are available so that we can get word about them to the Assyrians and they can get help." A staff member took over from him. He read off a list of various programs under way. He did so in a bored tone of voice, and in case I had failed to grasp his point, he kept prefacing each description with the words, "We do not help any particular group." Then the PRT chief and another of his staffers left, and there was just one officer left from the PRT. This man was pleasant. He listened to what I said about the Assyrian concerns. I happened to bump into him a few days later near the Convention Center. He looked serious and took me by the arm so that we could talk with no fear of anyone overhearing. "Let me give you a word of advice," he said. "Stop pushing us like this. No one is going to help the Assyrians. Stop trying to figure out who is in charge and how the system works. No one is in charge."

I was speechless. Absolutely no words came to mind to respond to this brutally honest and indeed cynical view of American economic aid policy in Iraq, the country that, with much fanfare, the Americans had "liberated" from Saddam Hussein. Apparently, the US government had just completely given up making any effort to ascertain what aid programs worked in Iraq, or indeed what aid programs there should be.

It was to be later on that we came upon the worst scenario. Finally we were able to get a list and descriptions of the various projects being carried out by the US government. We were stunned to see the tens of millions of dollars—in some cases, hundreds of millions of dollars—being given out for programs with broad goals. The "word on the street" in Baghdad was that much of the Iranian-backed insurgency was being funded with US dollars stolen from various assistance programs. Nobody seemed to be able to figure out where it was coming from. Putting two and two together—the massive amounts of funds being given out, the "nobody is in charge—we don't have the resources to follow up—we are just shoveling money out the door"—it appeared to me that in fact that the funds for these vaguely described programs such as "political consensus building" or "local governance standup" or "democracy building" were being used to fund the insurgency. This was later to be repeated during the Arab springs. And that was the reason that in spite of massive funding, the Iraqis could not see accomplishments on the ground. It was the most crushing display of American government cynicism and incompetence I had ever had the misfortune to witness. The officials we had spoken with couldn't help Christians but they stood by as millions of dollars went to fund the very enemies of all that was being done. My worst fears were confirmed months later when Peter Moore, working in one of the Iraqi government ministries, was freed after two years of captivity in Iran. He testified that the reason he had been kidnapped was because he had figured out and demonstrated the fact that large amounts of US and other international aid were being funneled to Iranian-based terrorists and being used to further their causes, while we couldn't seem to get any help for the Assyrians.

CHAPTER TEN

THE "ANGELS"

THE AMERICAN EAGERNESS to please and to reach out to all came to be seen by some of my Iraqi friends as a weakness. But others saw it as an obvious result of so many of the American service personnel in Iraq being Christian. Yet even if they weren't believers, the Americans we encountered were extraordinarily kind, generous, and considerate and this brings to mind "Ocean Cliffs."

Ask anyone who has spent any time in Iraq and he or she will tell you about Ocean Cliffs. This entirely banal sounding name—it might be a run-down boarding house somewhere between San Francisco and Eureka, CA—was in fact the makeshift office compound that the American military helping people inside the Green Zone moved to after the Convention Center was turned over to the Iraqi government. The offices that had previously been operating inside the cavernous Convention Center migrated, by necessity, to a large covered parking lot adjacent to the Convention Center, including the Iraqi Assistance Center. Portable office and housing units had been crammed into the parking lot because the US, despite turning formal government operations in Iraq over to the new Iraqi government, still had a lot to do on the ground in Iraq. Ocean Cliffs—the name had reportedly been coined with wry humor by British units— contained makeshift offices for everything from the Iraqi Assistance Center to the Armed Forces Network, to the United Nationals offices to a Combined Press Information Center. Long lines of people assembled at the entrance to Ocean Cliffs to have ID cards issues, get paperwork completed for refugee status, and so forth.

But, despite its makeshift and temporary appearance, despite its being an obvious ersatz version of the offices that had existed in the Convention Center before the transfer of sovereignty, I loved Ocean Cliffs. It was essentially located in the parking lot of the Iraqi parliament building. For some three months it was primarily my home because it had become so difficult to live outside the Green Zone and then get into it. Either I, or my relatives, might become endangered if I shuttled between their homes and the Green Zone where I tried to accomplish the various tasks I had taken on for the Assyrians. The only way to have accommodation inside the Green Zone on a commercial basis was to pay $220 a day at the Al Rasheed Hotel or to be embedded with the military at Ocean Cliffs. I opted for the bunk beds at Ocean Cliffs.

By comparison with the now non-functioning Convention Center, Ocean Cliffs was heaven. The facility was spotless and everything worked. The toilets worked, and were clean. The showers worked. The Internet worked. Next door, at the Convention Center, since the Iraqi government had taken over, absolutely nothing worked. Even at the Al Rasheed Hotel in the Green Zone across the street, nothing worked. At Ocean Cliffs the angels who made it work were just ordinary men and women of the US military. Their unassuming efficiency and unpretentious attitude of service often brought tears to my eyes, as it did to the Iraqis who watched them day in and day out.

At 4.00 a.m. every day, a woman US soldier opened the refrigerator that was part of the accommodation quarters, a room with six bunk-beds for reporters or other foreigners passing through the Green Zone, and filled it with fresh soft drinks. After this she set out breakfast supplies for anyone staying there: orange juice, muffins, cereal.

At 7.00 a.m. a cleaner would come and clean the room with the bunk-beds.

Later, there would be lunch, with a cafeteria-style service offering the opportunity for all-comers to chow down on basic American food. There were soldiers, military contractors, and others lining up every day, and none of them left hungry. There were all kinds of cooked food, from meat-loaf and hamburgers to french fries, salads, desserts and the other usual food offerings at cafeteria establishments in the US. One of the big ironies of Iraq, ranging from the UN to journalists to countries throughout the world as well as Iraqi opposition leaders enjoyed eating at the American cafeteria, shopping at the mini American shopping center inside the Green Zone and taking advantage of all the American amenities of a country they turned around and criticized so vociferously. In fact, the Ugandan security guards were among some of the foreigners working in Baghdad's Green Zone whose stomachs were not used to this cornucopia of rich food. Some of them had to be treated in the hospital for overeating. Regular Iraqis who worked for the Americans lined up to gawk at and enjoy the free food at lunch. No one had to pay a dime and it was there every day. For those of us who had, from time to time, eked out an existence on the fringes of Iraqi society, it was fit for a king.

At 6.00 p.m. they started serving dinner at Ocean Cliffs. Plastic boxes were available with meat, rice, vegetables, and more. In the evening also, Iraqi guards came over from their work-places at, say, the parliament building and begged for food. What was particularly pleasing about Ocean Cliffs was that the Internet worked flawlessly. By contrast, at the Al Rasheed Hotel or the Iraqi Parliament building, it didn't work at all, or sporadically at best. What really moved us was to see the goodness of the people running Ocean Cliffs, the young soldiers in charge of the Combined Press and Information Center, the people issuing badges, or interviewing refugees. It really was America at its best. The Iraqis who came to Ocean Cliffs, as they had to the Iraqi Assistance Center absolutely loved it. It was an oasis of calm and normalcy in the midst of chaos. When I was staying at Ocean Cliffs, it was being run by a National Guard battalion from Alabama. The young men and women angels could not have been nicer. If you had a TV that didn't work in the bunk-bed dorm room, someone would fix it. Was there a coffee-maker that wouldn't turn on? No sweat. You wanted help with the details of a story? The angels were there, always willing to help, always cheerful, and always caring.

By comparison, the Iraqi Media Center next door offered a depressing contrast with Ocean Cliffs. There were 25 brand new computers there, but none of them worked. To get a sandwich or anything as simple as a glass of tea, you had to bribe the employees. You need permission to get into some ministry? Forget it. You were banned.

As one might guess, the Iraqi journalists congregated not in their own press center but in the American-run press center at Ocean Cliffs.

While speaking of the incredible decency and generosity of ordinary American soldiers serving in Baghdad, I can't fail to mention "Baghdad ER."

I discovered what Baghdad ER was all about while I was staying at Ocean Cliffs and came down with a painful eye infection. The pain was so intense that I hardly knew how to function. I'd heard that there was a medical clinic run by the Americans in the Green Zone facility but had never visited it. I shuffled around to it and explained my situation.

Iraq certainly used to have widely admired medical facilities under Saddam Hussein. The corruption of the regime, however, the shortages imposed by the economic sanctions during the Saddam years, and then the chaos of the brief war of liberation itself had taken their toll. Nowadays in Iraq many people viewed hospitals as places where you went to contract diseases, not to get cured of them. But at Ocean Cliffs, the medical facilities in the clinic seemed like heaven on earth.

There appeared to be almost no patients, and I got full medical attention. Technically, Baghdad ER had been built by four Iraqi doctors—Modafar Al Shather, Kadim Shubar, Kasim Abdul Majeed and Clement Serkis—in the mid-1960s and named it the Ibn Sina Hospital. It was purchased for a fraction of its true value by the Iraqi government in 1974 for use by Saddam Hussein, his family and the Baath Party elite. I was amazed on entering Baghdad ER. It might have originally been an Arab-run hospital, but now it was run by the coalition forces. A plaque on the wall read, "Coalition forces in the spirit of the original founders of the Ibn Sina Hosptial provide excellent care to all, regardless of faith, creed, or color." Now here I was, sitting on a bed in a hospital room in the middle of Baghdad, listening as Dr. Dave Barry (no kin to the famous humorist) explained what he had diagnosed about my condition from a battery of tests.

Accompanying Dr. Barry on his rounds were two of the nicest, most delightful young Americans I have ever had the pleasure to meet, Lt. Leskanich and Sergeant Barkevich. As these angels treated me with great kindness and solicitude, they told me the stories of what kind of arrivals showed up at Baghdad ER: US soldiers who had been wounded on patrol in Iraq, regular Iraqis with urgent illnesses of various kinds, Iraqi mothers with sick children, even terrorists who had been in injured in shoot-outs with Iraqi or American forces. Everyone was treated with identical kindness and professionalism. "The Iraqis are always so grateful," said a young American attendant. "The terrorists who get brought here don't say anything. I am sure that they are shocked that we treat them as well as the others just minutes after they were trying to kill us." In the bed next to me was a terrorist that had just been brought in, and was being treated with the same kindness and care that I was. I can imagine the mixed feelings of those treating him realizing that he had just been trying to kill them, and here they were treating the wounds he had gotten from trying to do so. That was the height of their goodness—the fact that they could treat the very wounds that had been sustained through an attempt to kill them.

I had to spend the night in Baghdad ER and couldn't get over how moved I was by everyone's simple kindness and compassion. I kept wanting to say, "I just love these kids."

The world may choose to say what it wants about the US, but where in the world would you find people who liberate a nation, treat with compassionate medical care the people trying to do them harm, allow themselves to be criticized by those who know nothing, and dismiss their own efforts with a simple, "Just doing my job, sir, just doing my job."

I think I realize also why I was so moved at Baghdad ER. Goodness is at its most powerful when it is completely unassuming and the people exhibiting it act as though that it is simply normal life. Well it is not. A few weeks in Baghdad were enough to convince me of that.

If Baghdad ER and Ocean Cliffs were sources of kindness and joy not often found in the Middle East, I had one more occasion to see that God has his people everywhere. Guarding the Green Zone, for example, was a veritable army of different security agencies, most of them paid for by the US government. In addition to US military personnel—very often US Marines—cheerful crowd of security personnel, I noticed, were originally from countries like Uganda, the Philippines, Fiji and Peru. When I first went through a checkpoint manned by a Peruvian I noticed that, despite being in military uniform, he was wearing a cross. "Hallelujah," I said. I received back an echo greeting, "Halelujah." At other times the Peruvian guards who were committed Christians would respond, "Gloria Deos," or "Jesus Victorioso." I found that perhaps most of the Fijian, Ugandan, and Filipinos serving as security guards in the Green Zone were Christians and spontaneously made clear their faith to me. One day, I showed up at the Ugandan checkpoint. I said "Hallelujah," and the entire contingent of the Ugandan men and women stood up and said "Bless Jesus!" At this point, the head of the group suddenly took me aside, and I thought I had done something wrong. He put his hand on my chest and said, "So how many have you brought to Christ today?" "I'm not sure," I stammered.

"Brother," he said "If you cannot bring at least one person to

Christ a day, you will not be allowed through my checkpoint."
Then he burst into rollicking laughter.

Despite their openness—or perhaps because of it—such
brash speech did not please everyone in the Green Zone. A Fijian guard took me aside and asked for prayer for him and his
fellow-believers in the contingent. "We have a problem," he explained. "Many of us who are on duty in the Green Zone for
several hours each day have a time of prayer in our quarters in the
morning and then again at night. But the other day, the British
official in charge of us who works for the UN ordered us to stop
praying or we would be fired. I explained to him that we were
supplying security for the Green Zone and the people working
in it, but we ourselves felt the only type of security we had was
our time of prayer to God with the petition that he protect us.
I prayed for the contingent as he had requested and heard later
on that the British official had backed down, obviously realizing
how ridiculous he was being and in what a bad position he was
placing the UN.

The Green Zone in fact was a sort of phantasmagoria of different human groups in Iraq living out their particular attitudes
towards life. As the sun went down over the west of the city and
the dusk came on, the Muslim call to prayer could be heard from
countless Baghdad mosques. Close at hand was the clattering
of American armored personnel carriers and Humvees preparing to set off for their nighttime patrols of the city. The young
American soldiers were probably scared as they left the safety of
the compound to move into the dangerous Red-Zone parts of
the city of Baghdad. "We will be praying for you," I always called
out to them, and I'd invariably receive an enthusiastic thumbs
up sign. In the middle of the main open area of the Zone, Iraqi
guards would be lolling about, often ill-kempt and generally not

looking at all professional. On the other side of the Green Zone, where I would wait to be picked up and taken back to my accommodation, Filipino security guards would regularly gather into small choral groups and sing Christian hymns. Blended into the Muslim call to prayer and the clattering of the military convoys preparing to set out on patrol would be the sound of "Bringing in the sheaves, bringing in the sheaves, we shall all come rejoicing, bringing in the sheaves." To my amusement, the Iraqis at the checkpoints manned by Peruvians would join in the fun, responding to the Spanish "Hallelujah" with an Arabic-accented mimicry of the sound. Yet Iraq, in an odd way, was being touched by a different set of angels, an army of young people ardent about their personal faith from distant points on the globe such as Fiji, Peru, Uganda, and the Phillipines, and other parts of the world. There were also a very large number of American military personnel who, in contrast to some American bureaucrats, took their own faith with great seriousness and did their best to reach out to their fellow human beings in Iraq. One of the ironies was to come back to Washington, and while the simple question after meeting with the Iraqi prime minister or Iraqi president or any Iraqi government official in answer to "Would you mind if we prayed together?" was always welcomed. In Washington, the same question with a few rare exceptions would generate panic from the State Department to Congressional offices to just about anybody in between if you brought up the subject of having a short prayer together. It was like talking about the plague.

CHAPTER ELEVEN

GOODNESS WINS

HAS IRAQ FAILED? Have we lost Iraq?

After nearly 40 years of being a terrorist regime and thug state, and in spite of all the mistakes made in trying to create a new, free Iraq, the answer is a resounding no! Are there problems? Of course. As political Islam and socialism brought the worst forces together in Iraq, so America has given freedom and hope to not only Iraqis, but to all who suffer in the world.

For the first time in their lives, the Iraqi people have cell phones which they can talk on without fear. They can travel, get a passport, and buy a car—all impossible under the terrorist Saddam regime. Instead of the two "Saddam channels" that were available during the time of Saddam Hussein, now the average Iraqi has over 200 satellite channels that they receive every month free. They can watch television programs beamed from anywhere in the world, and use the Internet without fear. And for the first time in their lives they can go to school without having to study Saddam Hussein.

Is Iraq perfect? Far from it. As Braveheart said, the Iraqis are still suffering a collective Post Traumatic Syndrome Disease. There is still fear, brokenness and sadness. The reality is that a whole generation was lost. The hope is for the young generation that for the first time in their lives they can dream, they can start businesses, they can plan, they can do.

Iraq has a long way to go. The government still cannot shake its kleptocratic leanings. Thug rulers still hang around trying to milk the oil wealth. And the parliament does not represent the people, in particular the Assyrian Christians who have only one representative whereas they should have 25.

Even though problems are many, slowly and surely Iraq is beginning to stand up. In the reflection of postwar Japan and Europe, the dream of seeing Iraq turn into another miracle country, while not happening in the few months that the Iraqis dreamed it would, in a generation of political Islam and the influence of the neighboring terror state of Iran, Iraq as the second largest oil power in the world will stand up.

Did the over 4,488 American men and women give their lives in vain? Did the 33,184 injured sacrifice in vain?

NO!

It will take time, it might take a generation, but the liberation, the miracle of Iraq with the support of the free world will truly stand up and become a leader among the free nations of the world.

From day one, I along with the Iraqis began to fall in love. Having grown up in Japan and very anti-war, I would spit at the site of a military uniform. My father would tell me stories of the wonderful young men and women and the "angels" of a previous generation who rebuilt post-war Japan, but I had grown up in post-war Japan where the people hated the military for having taken the nation down a hole of death resulting in Japan's rampage across Asia and the death of over 3 million Japanese and the destruction of the country. The Japanese were born with a passionate hatred for anything military; they were equally passionate that Japan's constitution prohibiting any army or navy would be honored.

It was through this prism that I entered Iraq. Like the Iraqis, however, day by day my guard was taken down. I watched, along with the Iraqis, as the "angels" as we called them descended across the country. From the precious young woman who patiently listened to the stories of an Iraqi trying to find a relative to the older military man who wanted to build up a political system to those going out to patrol—I, along with the Iraqi people, was slowly falling in love.

Who were these kids? Why were they so good? Why did they care so much? Were they real? Was this possible?

Along with the Iraqis I found myself scratching my head in amazement at their consistent goodness. They were always positive. I would ask them, "What are you doing here?" They would answer to a man or woman, "Just doing my job, sir, just doing my job. Just want the 'aye-rackies' to have what we have." As amazing as it sounded, they really meant it.

From the cafeteria in the Al Rasheed to the checkpoints where they risked their lives every minute to the bus drivers to the sweet ladies who checked our ID cards, these were truly angels sent to bring joy and hope to the poor Iraqi people who more than they needed electricity and water and food, they needed hope, as they had done so many times before.

The Americans, young and old alike, who descended on Iraq in the days following the Liberation became our heroes. Grudgingly at first because they had been imbibed with so much hate from Saddam, it was fun to look out the window and watch the Iraqis begin to smile.

The highlight of our day was when the Americans came over to the Assyrian Center in their convoy of vehicles for only one reason—to ask if we needed anything. I sat in awe of these people. "So how are you all doing? Is there anything you need? Is there anything we can do for you" was always their greeting. With military-issue notebooks in hand, they would take notes as the Assyrians unleashed a torrent of complaints, never batting an eye and always smiling and saying, "OK, we'll do our best." They would be back in a few days with supplies, jobs for those that needed them, computers for the Women's Center, and food and toys for the residents.

We were falling hopelessly in love! Iraq as a nation, in spite of the best efforts of Iran, the terrorists, and all the evil Muslim forces, was falling in love with the angels.

One of the great heartbreaks of my life was to view a long display of names of those who had lost their lives in Iraq, many of whom I must have seen day to day, and knowing that they had paid the ultimate sacrifice for a people they didn't even know, but just wanted "the aye-rackies to have what we have."

I thought back to my precious parents who in the same mode had left their family, friends and a future to go to post-war Japan with nothing. Asking my dad why, he said simply, "Japan was having a hard time."

"But Dad," I protested, "you have been here for more than 60 years."

He replied just like the angels did: "I just wanted them to have what we have—faith in Christ and a better life."

Iraq has truly changed America as well. There are very few Americans who do not have a family member, a friend, or acquaintance that served in some capacity in Iraq. Ranging from TV dramas with story plots based in Iraq, to TV commercials offering services to help servicemen and their families returning from the war or affected by it and the liberation of 25 million people, has become part of the culture and daily life of America. Traveling the world I often bump into a service member either going to or coming from Iraq or Afghanistan. Whereas in the past I would have cursed them as "murderers" under my breath, I now cannot help myself from going up to them and asking where they are serving. Young men and women, with that familiar exhausted look in their eyes, answer with the familiar, "Serving in Iraq, sir." Without realizing what I am doing, I find myself hugging them and telling them "God bless you—we are praying for you. On behalf of the Assyrian Christians of Iraq, I want to thank you for liberating Iraq."

Why does Iraq matter? It matters for a very simple reason. Unfortunately evil exists in our world. I naively believed because I didn't see it in my own life that in the 21st century society had advanced to the point that people just didn't do such bad things anymore. It took me the shock of seeing the horror-stricken faces of my own flesh and blood living under Saddam Hussein's regime to realize that evil is with us. It took a good dose of reality to help me realize that there are "bad guys" in the world who just hate and are so evil that they cannot be talked to or negotiated with. I also learned something wonderful: In the face of unadulterated evil, there is still good in the world. I also learned first hand along with 25 million Iraq people that the America I once disliked for its arrogance and self-righteousness was in fact good.

What did America do in Iraq? It loved a people.

Walking down the street in Washington, DC, as I was completing this book I passed a middle-aged serviceman. "Where are you serving?" I asked him.

"Serving in Iraq, sir," he replied.

Without realizing what I was doing, I hugged him and kissed him. "Can I pray with you?" I asked.

Tears started to stream down his face and he said, "Thank you, thank you. I return in four days...I'm scared."

As we prayed together on that street in Washington, DC, across from the Capitol, he quietly said the words I have heard over and over: "I just love the Aye-Rackies. I just want to see them do well and have what we have."

Those words encapsulate the message of this book. Was he perfect? No, in fact he was scared, and he couldn't even pronounce "Iraqi." Did he love? Yes, he did! America has made many mistakes in Iraq. Many plans, programs and efforts failed. What did not fail, though, was the love of the best of America's men and women for a people they had never even met and couldn't even speak their language.

Like my parents a half century ago who went to Japan in a similar time, these "best and brightest" of America touched a nation, and that nation—reluctantly at first, and then with open gratitude—fell in love with them... the angels. To meet some of those angels in Japan, doing just what they had been doing in another country, I asked them "What are you doing here?" and as always they answered "Just trying to help sir, just trying to help."

My primary purpose in writing this book is so that in a small way, I, on behalf of the silent majority of Iraqis, and my people the Assyrians, can say "thank you" to America for liberating Iraq and to tell the story of how a country fell in love with America's best so that the precious families that sacrificed them for the liberation and freedom of Iraq can now know that it was not in vain, and these "kids" and their older partners truly have changed a country. They brought to Iraq what it needed the most—hope. Just as the Assyrian missionaries left from Mosul and Dohuk and Baghdad and other cities throughout the country to take Christianity to the world because it had been given to them, a new generation will surely go from the New Iraq to spread the gospel of freedom, hope and love that they have learned from the "angels."

***

To the American families of those who gave the ultimate sacrifice, on behalf of the silent majority of the Iraqi people, and my people the Assyrians, I would like to say, Thank you. Thank you for your sacrifice, thank you for your love and for your example. It will never be forgotten. One copy of this book, Liberating Iraq, *is being prepared for each American family who lost a family member in Iraq along with a letter thanking them for their service. It is also our goal to have a monument erected in central Baghdad dedicated to the "angels" who gave Iraq hope. A portion from the sales of each book will be donated toward the cost of providing the books to those families and to the monument. To participate, go to strategicmediabooks.com and enter code SMB7777 when you check out through Paypal.*

We are also gathering the stories of the nearly 500,000 "angels" who served in Iraq to compile in a follow-up book. If you have a story, please send it to info@assyrianchristians.com so we can include it in the upcoming book.